Christmas Sucks

What to Do When Fruitcake, Family, and Finding the Perfect Gift Make You Miserable

Joanne Kimes

author of *Pregnancy Sucks, Pregnancy Sucks for Men,* and *Dating Sucks*

adamsmedia
Avon, Massachusetts

Published by
Adams Media, an F+W Publications Company
57 Littlefield Street, Avon, MA 02322. U.S.A.
www.adamsmedia.com

ISBN 10: 1-59869-812-5
ISBN 13: 978-1-59869-812-1
Printed in the United States of America.

J I H G F E D C B A

Library of Congress Cataloging-in-Publication Data
available from the publisher.

This book is available at quantitydiscounts for bulk purchases.
For information, please call 1-800-289-0963.

dedication
To my daughter Emily.
The best gift I ever received!

contents

Chapter 9
It's Beginning to Smell a Lot Like Christmas 127

Conclusion:
The Big Day! 141

Resources 145

acknowledgments

Writing this book would suck a lot more without the help from these wonderful people: My talented editor, Meredith O'Hayre, the gifted designer, Michelle Kelly, my dear agent, Jeff Herman, and as always, Kate Epstein, who started it all. In addition, I'd like to thank Marisa Zafran, the public relations director at Le Parker Meridien hotel in New York. And finally, a big kiss to my wonderful husband, Jeff. Before we were married, Christmases were certainly a lot easier, but not nearly as much fun! I love you.

introduction

If you've had the courage to pick up this book, I applaud you. I'm sure there are plenty of holiday shoppers who'll read the title and think a book called "Christmas Sucks" is blasphemous. They'll think I deserve a one-way ticket straight to H-E-double toothpicks. I know this because my husband felt the same way when I told him that I'd be writing it. In fact, I was sure my next book would be entitled Divorce Sucks because of the all-out battles we had on the subject. It's not even that he's a deeply religious man. It's just that he believes that certain things should never be mocked.

I tried in vain to convince him that this book isn't about religion. It doesn't tease or put anyone down, except the generic mother-in-law because that's simply a given. In fact, one of the main points of this book is that we've lost the true meaning of Christmas somewhere between the Santa head Pez dispensers and the nativity scene made in the likeness of *The Simpsons*.

Besides, I'm no idiot. I realize that religion is a personal issue and as controversial as gay marriage, stem cell research, or who the heck Carly Simon's secret lover is in her song, "You're So Vain." I wouldn't dare debate such a heated topic, even though doing so may prove worthy of a guest appearance on the *Today* show. Instead, I choose to focus this book on the variety of overwhelming stresses that surrounds the holidays, and how to survive each one with your sanity, your family, and your bank account intact. True, with a book like this, I doubt Matt Lauer will beg me to come to Rockefeller Plaza, but at least I don't have to spend an eternity in hell. I tend to get cranky when I'm overheated.

So, if you've dared to read my book this far, perhaps you'll take a chance and read it further. If you're like me and dread the holidays despite the homemade cookies and that great version of "Santa Claus Is Coming to Town" by Bruce Springsteen, then this is the book for you. In it, you'll find dozens of tips on how to get through the holidays with enough Christmas spirit left over to bring a smile to your face. And, for no extra cost, you'll realize there's no shame in dreading the holidays and that there's nothing blasphemous about it. If you go to hell, it'll be your own damn fault.

So here's to all that is good and true and right about the holidays. I hope that with everything you learn from this book, yours will be a stress-free holiday so you can focus on what this most sacred day in Christianity is all about: Peace on Earth, good will toward men, and that great Bruce Springsteen song!

shop 'til you drop dead

For many, Christmas truly is the most wonderful time of the year, filled with loving family and friends, thoughtful gifts, and lifelong memories. It's a time of snowflakes and carols and free samples of summer sausage at Hickory Farms. Yes, December 25 is a great day that people look forward to all year long! At least some people that is. Most likely, these are the those of us who are under the age of eighteen and, dare I say, husbands who often leave the shopping and decorating and driving and entertaining to the wives while they sit on their asses all month watching sports (more on that good stuff later).

Many people actually dread December 25 more than they do April 15. And why shouldn't they? Both days are a pain in the ass to prepare for and both days cost a hell of a lot of money. And the stress! Man, the stress! The world becomes one big holiday moshpit with shoppers fighting over the last pair of Isotoner gloves, and groping any ass they can get their hands on during the annual office party.

The traffic's impossible, the malls are packed, the kids are home on school break, and the marital conflicts are more heated than those of Rosie O'Donnell and Elizabeth Hasselbeck. The only Christmas spirit you crave is the fifth of peppermint Schnapps you keep hidden behind the spare paper towels this time of year.

Face it. Somewhere down the line, Christmas has lost its meaning. It's no longer about worshiping the birth of Christ. Instead, it's more about keeping your head, and wallet, afloat while riding the Yule tides straight to total exhaustion. It's everything we can do to get through the relentless shopping, the constant housecleaning, the massive catering, the expensive decorating, the travel insanities, and the urge to drop kick our kids out the front door because they can't stop saying "we're bored." For many, Christmas is just a time to "get through."

But it doesn't have to be that way. In the pages of this book, you'll find oodles of ways to ease these holiday frustrations and come out the other end full of Christmas cheer that doesn't come from the bottom of that Schnapps bottle. Once you learn how to maneuver around the holiday obstacles, you'll find that Christmas really can be a time to enjoy, instead of just a time to just survive. With these skills in hand, you might even start looking forward to the holidays again, and that could be the Christmas miracle you've long been waiting for! So take a deep breath, pour some cocoa, and let's begin our holiday adventure. First up on our list, how to deal with the hellacious holiday chore of shopping.

Black (and Blue) Friday

If there's one day that marks the beginning of Christmas like no other, it's Black Friday, the day after Thanksgiving, when stores offer huge incentives to start off the madness of the Christmas shopping season. It's called Black Friday because it supposedly marks the day when stores turn their deficit (red) into profit (hence, black). What Black Friday means to you is a bevy of bumps or bruises from other holiday shoppers all pushing and shoving and kicking their way to the same GPS systems, designer clothes, and freaky-ass Bratz dolls that are on your gift list as well.

About 40 percent of retail stores' yearly business is done during the holiday season. It's like giving our economy a big chug of Red Bull, and stores will do just about anything to get you in there and boost their sales. They'll slash prices. They'll stage dress rehearsals to prepare for any and all problems that could slow down the shopping process. And they'll extend their hours so that you can shop around the clock. Oh boy!

Black Friday is the closest thing you can get to a holiday contact sport. You're lined up with over 100 million of your competitors on the first holiday shopping weekend, shoulder to shoulder, all waiting for the stores to open. As the sun inches up over the horizon, and your tummy digests that last bit of turkey and stuffing, the doors finally open, and the games begin. Adrenaline courses through your veins as the crowds pour onto the playing field. Ready . . . set . . . go spend your money!

If you've ever shopped on Black Friday, you've no doubt got the battle scars to prove it. The dent in your shoe where a rival stepped on it trying to beat you to the last Wii console. The snag in your sweater where another shopper's bracelet got stuck grabbing a Leapster out of your hand. Yes, Black Friday is the modern-day version of a Roman gladiator match, and you'd rather die than hand over that limited edition reindeer Chia pet.

Fortunately, you don't have to fight to the death any more. And you don't have to suffer through another Black Friday. You can still take advantage of great deals without ever leaving your house! That's because there are great savings online as well, and they continue on past the first shopping weekend when customers return back to work. In fact, a rather new phenomenon has emerged called "Cyber Monday" where shoppers can point and click their way to great savings while sitting at their desks. In 2007, over 700 million dollars was spent on Cyber Monday, where people got great savings without being pushed, shoved, or bruised, and often without paying tax!

If you want to start off the Christmas season and jumpstart our economy, put on your protective gear and head out to the mall on Black Friday. Or just put on your slippers and log onto your computer. Either way, you'll get great savings, the stores will be full of inventory, and you'll start the holiday shopping season out with a bang . . . hopefully not to your head!

"I went to my first Black Friday sale last week to save some money, but my suede pants were ruined when some kid brushed his ice cream cone against them. Considering how much I spent on those pants, I really didn't come out all that much ahead."

—Maddy

Baby, Can You Find My Car?

If you decide to brave the shopping malls, beware. Even though there are thousands of spots on the eight-tier parking structure, finding an empty one during the holidays is has hard as finding a good Ben Affleck film. Especially during peak times when the malls are as crowded as . . . well, not a Ben Affleck film. You circle the parking lot like a plane over O'Hare until the heavens part and the angels sing, and you find a car backing out of its spot! Oh joy and rapture! God's finally making it up to you for making you need braces! But hold on to your steering wheel, folks,—it's going to be a bumpy ride! Within seconds, drivers amass from nowhere hovering over your spot like vultures over a dying zebra.

If you're fortunate enough to be that lucky vulture and get that coveted spot, you pull in, and smirk at the other drivers who are green with envy. Aren't you Little Miss Lucky? Sure, you're on top of the world now, but you'll get yours in the end when you're done with your shopping and want to go home. Yes, hours later, when you've shopped till you've dropped, you'll head back to your car—and find it missing! Damn! Crap! Damn! One of those jealous drivers stole your freakin' car! Wait for it . . . wait for it . . . *bingo*! It hits you like a ton of fruitcakes: you're car's not stolen! With all the excitement of finding a parking spot, you forgot to notice where the hell you parked! You're completely and totally lost. Forget the TV show with the same name, being lost in a parking structure is where the real drama unfolds!

With no other choice, you traverse through the parking structure that winds around and around like asphalt intestines. Your legs ache and your heavy bags burrow deep in your finger joints. Just when you think you can go no further, you spot your car and suddenly remember that you parked right next to that bright red wall with the giant number three painted on it! You're saved!

Parking at the mall can certainly be a challenge this time of year. But there are a few tricks of the trade that can make it easier.

- Don't shop at peak times, when there are more shoppers than spots! (Duh.) Avoid lunchtime and weekends if possible. If you have to shop on the weekend, go early . . . even before the stores open. You may have to wait a bit, but waiting is far more enjoyable than driving around for a spot. Keep store catalogs in your car so you know what you want to buy before even going inside.
- Always write down where you parked on your ticket and take it with you! Duh again, but it's worth saying. If you often forget where you park, buy one of those key-ring voice recorders.
- If you have an outside antenna on your car, put something on it that'll make your car stand out. A rubber ball or even a handful of aluminum foil will do.

The Early Bird Catches the Inventory

Many people think they're "hip" and "with it." They know how to use a computer, program their TIVO, and even send a text message, albeit they spell out the whole word instead of using those clever little initials. But, as up-to-date as they think they are, they may be out of touch when it comes to the realities of how to shop for the holidays.

People can't shop like they did years back when there were fewer people to shop for and gifts didn't have to be so grand. Back then they'd put it off until the last minute and then do all their shopping on Christmas Eve. That method may have worked when people exchanged Pet Rocks as gifts, but it ain't gonna fly now. These days you have to get to the mall early if you stand a chance of having decent inventory left on the shelves.

Here's a quick rundown on how things go around Christmas time:

The Day After Thanksgiving: The stores are packed with people trying to get everything on their gift list when the sales begin, and be the most enviable (and most hated) shopper. There's plenty of sale merchandise in an ample selection of sizes and colors to choose from. There's even time to get something monogrammed.

The Second Week of December: The shoppers are still out en masse, but inventory is getting lower. First to be plucked clean are "medium" sizes, electrical gadgets, and anything seen on Oprah's favorite things show.

The Third Week of December: The stores have been picked over like lice on a monkey's head. The mannequins are naked because even the display items have been sold. Your best bet at this point is to hit the kiosks and grab a handful of pine-scented sinus pillows. If you were hoping to have something monogrammed in time for Christmas, get out your Sharpie.

Christmas Eve: The malls are a virtual wasteland of merchandise. All that remains are a few misplaced price tags and some errant buttons that roam through the stores like small, pearlized tumbleweeds.

As you can see, the secret behind successful shopping is to start *early*. Unless you have a lot of friends and family with sinus problems, you need to get your rear in gear. Make a list, check it twice, and head out to the mall. That way, when you're looking for the hot new video game that your grandkids told you they "need," it's actually in stock, and you don't have to buy it for twice what it's worth from evil stores and eBay merchants. And that robe you want for Uncle Al who continually greets you at the door with his boys hanging out, is actually in his size! Woo hoo!

When you shop early, your stress level is greatly reduced. You don't have to call all over the city desperately searching for an item, or go with the backup gifts that cost twice as much because you can't find what you're looking for. All you have to do is say "thank you" to the nice store clerk, and check one more item off your list of things to do. Life is gooooood!

Before you know it, your shopping will be done and you'll feel as relieved as you do after having sex with your husband and know you're off the hook for a few days. When your friends ramble on about how stressed they are with the holiday madness, just furrow your brow and nod your head in agreement. Deep down you'll revel in the fact that you've done all your shopping. Of course, you won't tell your friends that. You learned that lesson years ago when you bragged to other parents that your kid slept through the night as soon as he was born and suddenly your phone stopped ringing.

All's Fair in Love and Retail

Every so often, miraculous things occur such as a blind person suddenly being able to see, or Britney Spears actually wearing undergarments. And ever so often around Christmastime, another miracle occurs. That's when you walk into a store, and actually find one of the hottest selling toys still sitting on the shelf! In the '80s it was the Cabbage Patch Kids sensation. In the '90s it was the Beanie Baby boom. And in the last decade, the one thing everyone wanted was to get Bush out of the White House. Yeah, I know. It's not a toy, but everyone wanted it so it kinda counts.

Every year frustrated and determined parents go through hell trying to find the hot-ticket toy of the season so that their precious little kid won't be traumatized by being the only one on the block without this latest thing-a-ma-jig. It's the typical case of supply and demand. There isn't enough of this one item to go around, and, as anyone who's ever dieted or dated a noncommittal man knows, if you can't have something, you want it even more.

What happens is this: the parents of the future traumatized child will beg, borrow, steal, or blow somebody's effin' head off in order to get the one item they so desperately want. They'll drastically overpay for it on eBay. They'll wait in store lines for hours. They'll do whatever they can, no matter the cost or mandatory jail time, to give their sweet little bubalahs what they so dearly want on Christmas Day. Or at least what they want for a few hours until they get bored and play with the box it came in instead.

You'd think that toy manufacturers do this on purpose. That these SOBs don't make enough of these highly coveted toys just to start the whirlwind of chaos. But in

reality, they're just as frustrated as you are. They'd like nothing more than to produce and sell enough of the items to
go around and cash in on the sensation. But they can't. The
reason for the madness is that retail stores order their Christmas inventory months in advance so that it'll arrive in time
for the holidays. Since the stores don't know how well certain toys will sell, they order just what they *think* will sell
so they won't be stuck trying to unload a gross of Rudolf
bobble-head dolls come Presidents' Day.

Since the manufacturers didn't make enough toys to
meet the demand, and the stores don't have enough of them
to sell, you're faced with two options. One, wait in the long
lines, pay the exorbitant fees, and assault any shopper that
gets in your way, or, tell your kid that you're sorry but that
he just won't be getting the item that he so desperately
wants on Christmas morning. Sure, he'll be pissed, but life
is full of disappointing moments. Besides, even though your
kid may be desperate for a certain toy this year, my guess
is that if you did move hell and high water to get it, a few
weeks later, it'd be up on the high shelf along with the other
toys he desperately wanted last year but doesn't play with
anymore.

"I was at Toys "R" Us and saw two grown people having a fistfight
over a toy in the aisles. They were screaming and cursing and making
kids cry. I laughed in amazement, but then they saw me and I went
running in fear they'd come after me."

—Anne

I guarantee that when he gets older and thinks back on all his Christmas mornings, it won't be the gifts that he remembers; it will be the family and food and laughter and love. Just think back on your own Christmas mornings and you'll see what I mean.

Pony-Up Express

If there's one place I hate even more than the malls during the Christmas season, it's the post office. Actually, I hate it all year round and avoid it at any cost. I buy my stamps at the ATM, get my packing material at the drugstore, and if I ever have to mail a package, I simply stick a handful of stamps on it, and hope the neighbor's dog doesn't use it in lieu of the fire hydrant. But come Christmastime, when I have a lot of boxes to send, I have no choice but to head to the post office.

Just like at the malls, there are never enough parking spaces during the holiday madness, so I'm forced to park several blocks away and lug my awkward, heavy parcels with me. Keep in mind that not one of these gifts is for *my* side of the family—they're all for my husband's. And because my husband is one of those shopping procrastinators—and I have the sinus pillow to prove it—I'm forced to go to the post office at the last minute when the line out the door stretches endlessly like a beer line at a monster truck rally. I obediently take my place at the end and think of ways I can beat my husband without leaving a mark. I've heard meat in a sock works well. Gotta give that one a try.

The good news is that all three clerks are working behind the counter. Or at least they are for a few minutes. Then one goes off in the back and is never seen again. A few minutes later, a second precious postal worker puts up a "closed" sign and goes on break. And then there was one. And what a chatty Kathy she is, interviewing everyone about their holidays and cracking jokes. Great, I'm stuck in hell and Ellen DeGeneres is working behind the counter.

Finally, it's my turn up to bat! I hand Ellen my packages, and she gleefully informs me that, in order for my packages to arrive before Christmas, I have to overnight them. Yes, since my husband yet again ignored my pleas to get his act together early, we now have to spend more on shipping than the gifts actually cost. Here's a breakdown:

Gift for his parents: old family photos, recopied, and framed: $62.00

Overnight shipment and protective wrapping of said gift: $72.00

Telling him "I told you so, you dumb-ass moron!": Priceless

Learn from my mistakes. Most importantly, mail your packages early! For exact mailing deadlines, log on to *www. usps.com.* If you don't have time to use ground service, you'll be forced to overnight them, and that can be expensive. In 2007, a five-pound box sent before the mailing deadline cost $8.61. If it was sent after the deadline, that same package cost $56.64! Other mailing tips include:

- Use a sturdy box and seal your boxes with clear or brown tape (no duct tape). If your box is recycled, cross off old mailing information.

- Print the address in uppercase letters, don't forget the zip code, put your return address on the front of the package, and enclose the delivery address inside the gift as well.
- If you're mailing fragile items, be sure to wrap each one separately and mark "fragile" on the box. When sending perishables, be sure to mark such on the package so the recipient will open the box right away instead of two weeks later when your homemade fruitcake is hard as a rock . . . oh wait, bad example.
- Skip the post office entirely and have them come to you! Yes, you read me right! Recently, the post office announced the incredible news that with the help of a computer and a household kitchen scale, you can now send your boxes from the comfort of your own home! Go to *www.usps.com* and schedule a pickup.
- And, most of all, don't marry a shopping procrastinator, even if you could use a sinus pillow.

Chapter 2

all i want for christmas is my retirement account intact

No one will argue that the holidays can be expensive, and every year it seems to get worse. Relatives procreate and you have more family members to buy for. Kids leave a "one-teacher" elementary school for a "multiple teacher" middle school and there are more teachers to shop for. Promotions happen and you have new bosses to ~~brown nose~~ think of. Plus, during the month of December, you're suckered in by flashy displays, year-end sales, and severe guilt if you don't get that special someone a perfect gift. You're stripped of your budget-keeping will power and driven to near bankruptcy due to a force much more powerful than you. Case in point, in 2007, a major department store's motto was, "Don't just give a gift, grant a wish." Now, a gift isn't even good enough anymore. We're expected to fulfill a damn dream! No wonder our nation is in debt.

On average, a family spends over $900 on gifts alone during the Christmas season. Then there are the other holiday expenses, such as travel, parties, charities, holiday decorations, and many more. Yes, it's beginning to look a lot like Christmas, and it's beginning to cost a freakin' arm and a leg!

But it doesn't have to be that way. Just because it's time to cough up the Christmas cash, doesn't mean you have to dip into the college fund and pray your kid's only smart enough to warrant trade school. There are plenty of cost-cutting ideas and money-saving methods to get you out of your hole and back on strong financial footing. That way, when the holidays are over, you actually *will* grant a wish—a wish to yourself that, come January, you won't get a visit from the repo man!

The Christmas Pad

It happens every year. Christmas is over and you can't imagine where all your money went. You budgeted for the gifts and the tree, but somehow your bank account is as empty as Jessica Simpson's head. The problem is that, although you budgeted for the big-ticket items, there are lots of hidden holiday expenses that add up rather quickly. For instance, when you planned your holiday budget, did you take into account the family portrait needed for the holiday cards, the fancy metallic pen to fill them out with, and the extra postage needed to mail them? What about the new clothes for the holiday parties, the hostess gifts, and the babysitter to watch your kids while you're at the party? Or the cost of the traditional Nutcracker tickets, the parking, and the souvenir program? Did you account for the long-distance calls to friends and family and the extra gas to visit those closer by? What about the holiday wrapping paper, bows, batteries, extension cords, garlands, mistletoe, festive new tablecloth, and adorable Santa plates that you couldn't resist at Pottery Barn? And let's be honest, what about all the stuff you bought for yourself when you're out buying for others?

There was an interesting study done by USAtoday.com in 2004. They added together all, and I mean all, of the holiday expenses of a typical four-person household, from the Christmas tree to the gift for the father-in-law to the family holiday movie (including the buttered popcorn) when the kids are on school break. When it was all added together, the grand total was (drum roll please) $4,906 (gulp!).

The one lesson to learn from all this (besides that Pottery Barn really has some irresistible dishware) is that when you make a holiday budget, you need to pad on extra for the incidentals. Calculate how much you're going to spend on the obvious things, and then tack on an additional 20 percent. It's also important to keep a running tally of your December spendings so that you know right away if you're going over budget. Not only so you can cut back, but so you can avoid moving back with your parents when next month's bill arrives.

Once Christmas is over and you've bought everything you needed, tally up your list and pack it away with your Christmas decorations. That way next year, when the holiday season arrives, you'll know exactly how much you spent the previous year and how much you should budget for this one. Once you realize it's the small things that add up, you'll be better prepared to face the holidays and have a much fuller bank account come next year. Jessica's head, we can only hope.

Join the Club

It doesn't take an accountant to tell you that the reason we go into debt in December is that we spend money like it was going out of style. Every time we turn around we open our wallets and put even more debt on our credit cards. If only there was a way to save the money you'll need in December throughout the whole year. If they can put a man on the moon, and make a bra that both lifts and supports, you'd think this would be a breeze.

What, you say? They *have* done this? Let me do a little research. I'll be right back. . . . Oh yeah! You're right! You're quite the smarty pants! It seems that most all banking institutions and credit unions have something called a "Christmas fund account." In fact, it's one of the most popular savings plans around and more common than your bank charging a fee every time you turn around.

Because you're required to make a deposit every month in a Christmas account, often automatically from your checking account, you won't even think about it until, come December, you'll have enough money to cover your holiday expenses. And because there are often penalties for early withdrawal, you tend to leave the funds right where they are. What a good little saver! True, these accounts don't offer a high rate of interest, but when you factor in how much interest you'd pay on your credit cards if you charged your expenses and couldn't pay them off right away, you come out way ahead.

These savings plans aren't just limited to Christmas either. You can use them for any important event, whether it be another celebration of any nature, your annual nudist colony retreat, or a Hummer if you're environmentally unfriendly and have a small pee-pee. These funds are non-specific and, unlike me, nonjudgmental.

True, if you're one of those disciplined people who can automatically put your latte money aside for the holidays, you don't need any specialized savings plan. But for the rest of us mere mortals who lack the organizational skills, the discipline, and the will power not to blow all our savings on a new set of golf clubs, then a Christmas savings account is just the plan for you!

Teen Trouble

You knew going into the deal that it'd cost a hell of a lot of money to raise children. In the early years it was for diapers and pre-school. As they got older it was for cars and rehab. But as much as you were aware of the basic costs of raising a kid, I bet there was one expenditure you never saw coming: the astronomically high price of buying Christmas presents for teenagers.

By the time your babies are old enough to produce body odor, they can't be appeased with trinkets like stuffed animals and Lego sets. Once they've entered teen-hood, they've gotta have all the stuff the other kids have or else they'll simply die! Some of the things on their must-have lists include iPods (with video screen), laptop computers (with Bluetooth technology), and designer clothes (that you can't even afford to buy yourself).

These days it's not keeping up with the Joneses that causes such financial havoc. It's keeping up with the Paris's and Lindsay's and every other teen idol that carries a tiny dog in their designer purse that costs more than your home mortgage. Granted, teenagers have always needed someone to emulate, but why can't they choose someone known for doing good instead of someone known for doing rock stars?

"Every year we go all out on Christmas for our teenagers, spending way more than we should trying to make them happy. And every year it works for like three hours and then they go back to their usual surly selves. When will we ever learn?"

—Devon

Forking over the dough to buy this crap is especially hard when your kids are awkward teenagers instead of cute little toddlers. Their once innocent eyes have transformed into ones that roll up in their head whenever you speak. And their once high-pitched voices that sounded as if they just sucked on a helium balloon are now deep and cracking and bark out orders whenever they want something. "Hey, Mom! Billy just got surround sound in his room and I want it too!"

In addition, now that they've entered the double-digit age, the magic of Santa Claus is gone. Not the magic of how Santa can fly around the world in one night, but the magic of how to get your kid to do whatever you want with a single threat of coal. Gone are the days when your kid misbehaved and, in just one Santa warning, he'd fall right into line like a holiday Rockette.

If your children are still babes in the wood, take my advice and stash the cash. Not only for Christmas gifts, but for the oodles upon oodles of unexpected expenses that you never saw coming. Take the prom for instance. Did you know that it's now commonplace for girls to want their hair and makeup professionally done, complete with extensions and eyebrow waxing? And that they insist on wearing a designer gown and having a professional portrait taken as well? It seems that the prom is the new wedding—even worse because at least with a wedding, your kid moves out when it's over.

If you're not financially equipped to keep up with all the "must haves" of today's kids, perhaps just get them one thing on their must-have list and give them a coupon for something else that you'll get after Christmas when everything is half off. Or, what about pushing the overpriced pendulum in the other direction and get them less expensive gifts that offer family quality time like some DVDs of their favorite movies you can all watch together. Or, how about just *one* hot new computer game, and a board game. Then, you can start family game night. Sure your kids will be pissed, but perhaps, just perhaps, these nights will actually be fun. You'll get to have family time, and they'll learn they can actually communicate outside of a chat room. Of course, don't expect your kids to admit to it. They'd never reduce themselves to such a level. But don't be surprised if, when they have their own kids, they'll continue on with this tradition.

Money Is the Root of All Evil Fighting

Couples fight. They just do. Well, maybe not all couples. Perhaps there are some lucky few who talk things over, work out a compromise, then rub each other's feet while listening to a best of Yanni CD. But I gotta believe that life evens out in the end and these people never buy winning lottery tickets or get those really great parking spots right in front of the building.

When it comes to the most common topic of domestic disputes, the majority of surveys and Oprah shows claim that the bickering centers around money. And since the holidays are a time of spending great wads of it . . . ipso facto light bulb moment . . . it can be a time of great marital discord as well.

Of course, money disputes are common all year round. But during the holidays, when money is at a premium and patience is at a minimum, fights seem to increase with intensity. What adds the most gasoline to the already blazing fire is when you have a different manner of spending money than your spouse. When it comes right down to it, there are actually three distinct belief systems on how to spend, and if you're not in sync with your mate, it can lead to financial disaster. The three spending habits are as follows:

1. You and your partner are both big spenders: You don't care how much something costs. If you want it, you buy it. This type of philosophy results in far fewer arguments—although far more second mortgages.

2. One of you is a big spender and the other one is more frugal: This is where the real conflicts lie, since it's hard to agree on how much to budget for Christmas when one of you believes in big purchases and the other believes in big discounts. When you both come from opposite ends of the spending spectrum, it's hard to find a common meeting ground.

3. Both you and your main squeeze don't like to spend: Whether it's because you don't have the money, or don't want to spend it, this type of set up will give you the least amount of battles and of course, the least amount of bills.

If you and your spouse don't see eye to eye on dollars and cents, you may not have the merriest of Christmases. Sure, you can try to be logical and base the amount of money you'll spend on how much spare money you have, but when are people logical when it comes to money? Go to your closet and count how many pairs of shoes you own and you'll see what I mean. Besides, when it comes to a Christmas present, its monetary value can mean a lot. Friends and family may see it tied in with how much they're loved. Coworkers may see it tied in with how much they're valued. And a new girlfriend sees it tied in with whether or not her fella is gonna get lucky. Because there can be more to a gift than meets the eye, deciding on how much to spend on a gift can be far from logical.

If you and your significant other have significant issues over money, try to compromise. For instance, if you don't want to spend a fortune on a tree but he has his mind set on a ten-foot Douglas fir, get that ten-foot beauty at a home goods store instead of an overpriced tree lot, and buy it as close to Christmas day as possible, since prices tend to go down week by week. If you want to get your folks an expensive Italian espresso machine because you still feel guilty about having them pay for your third year abroad when all you did was have sex with your gorgeous French boyfriend, skip the kitchen specialty store and look for deals online (see page 27 for tips). And if one of you wants to go all out on a gift for a boss, see if you can write off the expense (just don't make it too nice or your boss will think he's overpaying you). As you can see, there are many ways to rationalize an expense—just think back on some of the things you told yourself before you bought all those shoes.

A Christmas Tip for You

I can't talk about hidden holiday expenses without mention-
ing the ever-popular and ever-expanding tradition of tipping.
Even when it's not the holidays, tipping is still encouraged
for everyone from an Appleby waitresses to the Z-Gallery
deliverymen. But when Santa comes around, there are so
many palms to grease it's like everyone's walking around
with a handful of Crisco.

This time of year, there are plenty of lists stating who to
tip and how much to give. And since this is a book on how
to get through the holidays, I'll include a list here to save
you from having to find it elsewhere. Keep in mind these
prices are only a guideline. The rates will vary depending
on where you live and how generous you want to be. Me,
I resent giving out Christmas tips entirely as well as the
whole tipping process. Inevitably, I'll put money in the Starbucks tip jar and he just stands there looking at me without
even uttering a "thank you." Or, I'll put the tip in the jar
just as he turns around and doesn't see it. Should I tell him I
tipped him, which makes it look like I'm fishing for thanks?
Or not say anything, have him think I'm a cheapo, and run
the risk of getting spit in my morning cappuccino? It's all
too stressful. But if you're a fan of the whole process, here are
some basics of how holiday tipping works:

Regular babysitter: One to two night's pay, plus a small
gift from your child.

Full-time nanny: One week's to one month's pay based
on tenure, plus a small gift from your child.

Personal trainer: $50 to $100 depending on how often
you use them, or how much they yell at you.

Dog groomer: ¼ to ½ cost of a session.

Your housekeeper: one week's pay.

Gardener: one week's pay.

Your regular USPS mail carrier: Noncash gifts with value up to $20.

Apartment building superintendent: $30 to $150. Tip less if you tip throughout the year.

Apartment doorman/concierge: $10 to $80 or more each, depending upon the building. If you don't have many doormen, you can tip each one more.

Apartment building handyman: $15 to $40 each.

Apartment building elevator operators: $15 to $40 each.

Manicurist/pedicurist: $15 or more (opt for more if you have gross feet)

Hairstylist: The cost of an appointment.

Newspaper carrier: Daily: $15 to $25, weekend: $5 to $10

Teacher: $10 to $100 depending on how many teachers your kid has, and how good you want their grades to be!

School crossing guard: $10 to $20

Coaches, tutors, ballet instructors, music teachers: A small gift from your child.

While I know it's common to tip the people in your life, I think some of these people oughta tip you as well! Sure, they're the ones that provide a service, but you have a role in the deal too. On that note, here's my own list of holiday tips that *you* should receive:

Your hairdresser: The cost of one appointment for being a loyal customer and not cheating on them with another beautician, which is an all too common practice.

Your gardener: The equivalent of one flat of pansies to make up for the ones he mowed over despite your efforts to put sticks around the edge of the flowerbed.

Your babysitter: The price of restocking your fridge.

The cable guy: The equivalent of half a day's pay to compensate for the hours you waited for him when he promised to arrive between 9 and 12 and finally showed up at 3:05—the following day!

The cleaners: The price of one silk blouse to replace the one they said was damaged when you brought it in when you know darn well it wasn't and you never won that battle.

Your husband: The cost of one night with a prostitute because of those nights when you didn't feel like doing it but did it anyway.

How to Save Money During the Holidays

Now that we've seen all the monetary pitfalls that could bury you waist deep in debt, the question remains, "How can you cut back on holiday expenses and still have enough money to go around? Good question. And to that, I'll provide some good suggestions:

Shop year round for people you know will be on your gift list whenever there's a good sale.

Take advantage of Internet savings. If you know where you want to shop, go to Google.com and type in the store name and then "promo code" or "coupon" (e.g., Disney promo code coupon). Also, if you have a specific item in mind, Google it and then type promo code or coupon (e.g., American Girl promo code coupon). Sometimes you can even get more than one discount per shop. Recently, I went to Disney.com and ordered $80 worth of gifts and got $27 worth of discounts. Then I did the same thing for Victoria's Secret and ended up with free shipping, a $15 discount, and a free tote bag that normally costs $15! You can also go directly to Web sites such as slickdeals.com, currentcode. com, cheapuncle.com, and findsavings.com to see what coupons they have available at specific stores or for specific products. Finally, there are always deals on Web sites such as overstock.com and half.com.

If you're in a store looking for a big-ticket item and want to be sure you can't get it for less online, call 1-888-Do-Frucall (you have to register first at *www.frucall.com*). Then punch in the bar code number and you'll be told where it may be sold for less online, and how much it costs. Then, you can either purchase the item online, or see if a store can match the price.

Do a secret Santa. My holidays used to be very affordable but then I had to ruin a good thing and marry a guy with more family members than al-Qaeda. If you come from a large family, suggest doing a secret Santa. True, you won't get as many gifts come Christmas, but 'tis better to save than to receive.

Buy gifts in bulk and then wrap them as individual gifts.
Many potential gift items are packaged in groups such as a case of
wine, a boxed set of books, or a set of dishes. Places such at Costco
or Sam's Club are a great place to find items sold in bulk.

If you get an electrical gadget, pass on the extended warranty. In most all cases, even if it breaks down, you still
come out ahead paying out of pocket to get it fixed.

Make some gifts. People are especially touched when you
put time and effort into a gift. Even if it's crap, they still
say "Awww." If you can cook, the sky's the limit with items
such as homemade jam, breads, and sweet treats. If you can't
cook, you can still create a nice gift. This year, I'm giving out
infused vodka. It's easy to make, looks great in a pretty bottle,
and who couldn't use a stiff shot this time of year! (For more
info on infused vodkas, go to *www.cocktailstimes.com*.)

Give the gift of time. Make up a coupon offering to baby-
sit, help out in the garden, paint a room, run an errand,
whatever you think the recipient might need help doing.

**Although not always the case, stores often offer better
discounts on Wednesday and Thursday** if they need to
make up for weaker sales during the beginning of the week.
The deals can get even better on the weekends if sales during
the week have been really slow.

**Look for price protection plans where you shop and
keep receipts.** It may be possible to bring the receipt back
to the store after the holidays and get money back if the gift
you bought goes on sale.

If you can't lower the amount of money you're going to spend on the holidays, lower the amount of money you're going to spend on nonholiday things. Brown bag it for lunch at work and you can save about $200 in a month. Rent a movie instead of going out. If you need something around the house, go to Craigslist.com or freecycle.org where you can get things for free. Cut grocery coupons and shop at stores that'll double them. If you can't give up your morning Starbucks experience, just order a small drip instead of a grande latte. You may think these are small cuts, but when you add them together, they can add up to huge savings.

Negotiate! Talk to the sales managers or store owners (never the sales clerks) and see what kind of deal you can get. Ask for display items or something that has a small scratch or flaw, offer to pay in cash, or see if you can get a reduction if you buy several items from that one store.

If you pay for holiday items on your credit card, pay it off quickly. It's been estimated that 30 percent of shoppers won't pay off their Christmas debt for twelve months, which can add approximately $175 to an initial $900 expense. If you have credit card debt, call your credit card company and see if you can negotiate a lower interest rate. If you have two cards with debt, pay off the one with the higher interest rate first. Also look into transferring the debt from the higher-interest card to the card with the lower interest. Resist getting store credit cards to get a one-time price cut since, if you can't pay it off right away, they usually have interest rates of over 20 percent!

Have a pre-Christmas garage sale when there are lots of shoppers looking for cheap stuff, and use the cash for holiday gifts.

If you haven't shopped slowly throughout the year whenever there's a good sale like I suggested, and you have a lot of gifts to buy, shop for them as close to Christmas as you can. Although this goes against everything I believe in for having less stress during the holidays, you will find deeper price reductions.

Relax and Recoup . . . the Savings!

One last quick thing. Did you know that if you're stressed out during the holidays, it might actually cost you money? When people are stressed, it sets up a lot of potential expenses. People tend to eat more, which translates to higher food costs, bigger clothes to buy, and more doctor's bills to deal with medical issues like diabetes, heart issues, and even gum disease. Insurance premiums rise as the scale goes up too, often twice as high for someone that's obese. When you're stressed, you also spend more money on alcohol. And don't forget the costs for prescription antianxiety pills. Being stressed can make you physically sick, so you spend more money on over-the-counter cold and flu remedies and lose money in lost wages when you need to stay home. If you miss a lot of workdays, you may even get passed over for that big promotion.

"Every year it's always the same. I run myself ragged during the holidays doing everything that needs to get done and then I get sick on Christmas Day and have to spend it in bed. What's the point?"

—Gwen

If you find yourself stressed out during the holidays, and who doesn't (unless you're a kid or a husband), take a deep breath instead of a cold beer. Skip the potato chips and go for a walk. Or take a hot bath to decompress instead of a hot toddy. The goal is to relax the healthy way. Not only will exercise and relaxation calm you down, but it will also keep you, and your investment portfolio, going strong!

Chapter 3

here comes santa claus:
ho ho hold me back!

Call him what you want: Santa Claus, St. Nicholas, Father Christmas. As with anyone who leads a life of secrecy, he goes by many aliases. Sure, he has your kids fooled into thinking he's the holy grail of the holidays, but to you, this jolly old man spells nothing but trouble. He's just the man in red who steals your thunder. Your kids give him credit for the gifts you killed yourself to get. They clamor to cuddle on his lap, while the only physical attention you get is when they wipe their runny nose on your sleeve. And they'll write him a long, thoughtful letter with lots of pretty pictures, when all you get for Mother's Day is a quick scribble of a note. Yeah. He's trouble all right.

Unfortunately, if you have kids, there's no way getting around the big guy during the holidays. You'll just have to accept it like other unpleasant inevitables such as death, taxes, and your husband requesting a three-way. But, even though you can't escape the big man in red, there are some ways to navigate around him. Read and learn.

No, Virginia, Of Course There's No Damn Santa Claus

If there are two words that epitomize the essence of Christmas, it's the words, Santa Claus (actually, there are others, like "account overdrawn" and "gridlock traffic" but we'll stick to the issue at hand). This jolly old man has been a part of your holiday culture since infancy, but I'll bet you never knew much of when or where he came from. So, in the interest of full disclosure, and to help reach my word count required for this book, allow me fill you in on the background of this elusive man.

Spoiler Alert: If you still believe that a man old enough to be a card-carrying member of the AARP climbs down your chimney and puts gifts underneath your tree, skip this section! Some things, like the history of Santa and the ingredients of a hot dog, are better left unknown.

According to my intense research, which consisted of surfing the Internet while checking on my gossip sites, I've discovered that there actually *was* a Saint Nicholas. He was a bishop in the fourth century in what is present-day Turkey. Like his modern-day namesake, Saint Nicolas was also a generous man. But instead of handing out baby dolls and Sony PlayStations to good little boys and girls, his efforts were focused mainly on the poor. In fact, he was best known for giving dowries to three impoverished daughters so they wouldn't be forced to pursue a career in prostitution.

Meanwhile, somewhere back in pre-Christianized Germany, a tradition began of children putting their boots near the chimney on a cold winter's night, and filling them with straw, sugar, and carrots for the flying horse of their folklore god, Odin. In exchange, the children would wake up to discover that Odin had rewarded them with gifts and candy. Years later, after the German's adopted Christianity, this tradition became associated with Saint Nicholas, since both Odin and the saint were old men with soft, white beards.

As Christianity spread, other countries threw in their two cents about the tale of Saint Nicholas. Some dressed him in a long, green robe. Others had him riding a goat. And still others thought him to be an elf (thus explaining how he could scale down a narrow chimney). Even his name was the blending of Saint Nicolas and the Dutch name for their own revered bishop, Sante Klaas. But it wasn't until 1823, when the famous poem, "A Visit from Saint Nicholas" (later to be renamed, "'Twas the Night Before Christmas") was written, that Santa got his updated look and reindeer sidekicks.

To cement the deal, in 1931 Coca-Cola was trying to change its image. Before 1903, Coca-Cola was used for medicial purposes to give sick people a boost. Since its active ingredient was cocaine, it easily achieved its goal (later, the cocaine was swapped out with caffeine). During the Depression, sales plummeted and it was the profits that were in need of a boost. Coca-Cola stopped catering to tired adults and changed its image to a wholesome family drink. As a marketing ploy, they commisioned well-known Chicago illustrator Haddon Sundblom to paint a humanlike Santa Claus based on the famous poem. Using his neighbor, Lou Prentice, as a model, Haadon created Santa's classic appearance. Coca-Cola went all out and even printed the ad in color, an anomoly at the time since almost all ads were black and white. As anyone who's seen that classic moment when

Dorothy enters Munchkinland knows, color is a powerful tool! The ad was a huge success, and the world fell in love with that roly-poly man (and families fell in love with that bubbly beverage, causing sales to soar! Gotta love marketing).

So that's it, folks. The history of Santa Claus. He's gone through quite a transformation from his early days of saving young women from becoming whores. And chances are, he'll continue to be around for many more years to come, outliving most other hearty life forms, such as cockroaches and Cher. So the next time you see Santa, take a minute to reflect on his past and appreciate his appearance. Although if Haddon Sundblom had lived next door to a guy that looked more like Brad Pitt, I bet both kids and grown women would be clammering to sit on his lap!

Smelly Claus, Smelly Claus

Sometimes it's not the kid who's panicked by the sight of Santa, but rather the parent. And not because they too suffer from coulrophobia (the clinical name for fear of clowns, mimes, and all other costumed characters such as Batman, Snow White, and the big Kahuna himself, Santa Claus), but rather because most of the Santas they encounter don't resemble the perfectly cast jolly old men they see in family films and Macy's Thanksgiving Day parades. Instead of a man with rosy cheeks and sparkly eyes, the average run-of-the-mill mall Santa looks like he's been ridden hard and put away wet. His beard reeks of cigarettes, his clothes smell like mothballs, and his lap has more pee stains than the sidewalks of South Central L.A. Yes, you can bet that your local

Santa won't resemble the crème de la crème of Kris Kringles, but rather the scum that builds up between his toes. As you cautiously place your kid down on his lap, you silently pray he won't pick up a nasty disease like the ones you can get from a public toilet seat.

This time of year, the need for Santas is high, and the inventory of elderly men with their faculties in tow, a soft, white beard, and a belly large enough to rival that of a contestant on *The Biggest Loser* is low. Those hiring Santa Clauses figure that any wino, homeless person, or man living off of sperm bank donations will suffice. For all you know, the "Santa" you're handing your precious baby to is someone wanted in all fifty states. Sure it's Santa, the symbol of trust, but can you really trust someone who hides a bottle of scotch in his beard?

The good news is that your child is young and naive and far less judgmental than we grown ups. I'll bet he's never been grossed out by your morning breath or belittled you for singing his evening lullaby off key. The innocence of children is a beautiful thing, and it's a shame we lose it as we get older. If we didn't, just think of how much nicer the world would be without judgment, racism, or those Joan and Melissa Rivers post-Oscar shows.

Because of the innocence of youth, it's easy to explain why Santa doesn't look exactly like he does in a book. If your child asks why Santa's beard pulls off and he smells like dog food, give him the excuse parents have been using throughout the ages: "This isn't the real Santa, sweetie. This is one of his helpers. Santa's so busy making toys, he can't be everywhere." They always seem to go for that one.

One day, sooner than you'd like, your child will grow up and not want to sit on Santa's lap anymore, and this will all be behind you. Until then, use the "Santa's helper" line, and one of those sanitary paper toilet seat covers on Santa's lap. Your child will be happy, his crotch will be safe, and all will be right with the world.

Secret Santa or Santa's Secrets

As a parent, you want to be honest with your children. You tell them that monsters aren't real, that their flu shot may hurt, and that a stork brought their new baby brother (you can only take honesty so far!). But, when it comes to being truthful with your kid, there are a few loopholes in the system where honesty cannot permeate. Those loopholes include such mythical creatures as the Easter Bunny, the Tooth Fairy, and of course, Santa Claus. With these loopholes in place, the only option you have as a parent is to be a liar, liar, pants on fire.

From the moment your kids are born, you tell them the enchanting tale of how Santa Claus comes down your chimney at night bringing gifts to all the good little boys and girls. You want them to believe in the magic of Christmas just like you did as a child. It all seems so harmless. But as they get older, and are able to speak, the questions start coming. "But we don't have a chimney, Mommy." "Well, honey, Santa has magic powers and can go through walls if there isn't a chimney."

Then your kid goes to school, where math is learned and logic is encouraged. What started out as a series of innocent fibs has escalated into a web of lies so big it could entrap a Dodge Caravan. Answering their questions now requires a degree in physics! "But Mom, I don't get it. If Santa eats one cookie and drinks a glass of milk at every house, he'd down like 20,655,000,000 calories and gain like 2,950 tons. How come he doesn't, huh?"

Here's another good one:

"Hey, Ma, since there are 378 million kids that live in 92 million homes, Santa'd have to cruise like 3,000 times the speed of sound to deliver his toys . . . assuming of course that he travels east to west to take advantage of the time zones. How come he can go that fast without burning up? Huh, mommy? How?"

And then there's my favorite:

"Pop, if each toy weighs a couple of pounds, that'd mean his sleigh would carry 321,300 tons. But I just learned a reindeer can only pull 300 pounds each, so there'd have to be like 2,142,000 more reindeer. How come we never hear about them, huh Daddy? And what are their names?"

Man, who says public school systems suck? As you can see, it gets harder and harder to lie to your kid about Santa. But even though they get older and lose their chubby cheeks and plump little fingers, we continue the façade as long as we can. Not so much because we want our kid to believe anymore, but because we're afraid of being caught. They'll realize that we've lied to them for so many years, and it's just no fair because if they lie to us, they get grounded!

Personally, I hate lying to our nine-year-old daughter. I would like nothing more than to put an end to this scam and tell her the truth, but my husband is a Santa Nazi. He was raised in a very small town where children believed in Santa years longer than most average kids. He thinks it's sweet. I think the town must be located near a power grid. If my husband has his way, our daughter will believe in Santa Claus when she walks down the aisle. In fact, if our daughter ever finds out that Santa isn't real, he'll insist on moving out of our big city and back to his small town where there are no shopping malls, no movie theatres, and no gourmet coffee.

According to a recent study, the average age that a kid discovers the truth about Santa is 8.3 years. Like the average age of menstruation, this figure too is getting younger. Kids are savvier with Internet access and cable TV. Plus, oftentimes they discover the truth but don't let on because they don't want you to know they know for fear of ending the gravy train of cool gifts. So they lie to you about knowing the truth, figuring you deserve it for lying to them! Told ya they're smart!

The Jig Is Up

Finally, after all those years and all those lies, your kid finally asks you point blank, "Do you get me the presents, or does Santa?" Unlike with other questions, like "Is Santa real?" or "Do you believe in Santa," you can't be ambiguous. You can turn the tables and say the typical, "What do you believe?" or just give the fall-back, "He's real if you think he's real" crap. But with a point blank question, you freeze like a deer in headlights and ponder if you should tell or not, wondering if your kid will be traumatized or your spouse will pack up the family. You realize if you tell, you'll never have your innocent child back or be able to blackmail your kid to clean up his room because Santa is always watching. Plus, if you have younger kids, you'll then have to turn your older kid into a liar too so as not to spill the beans. And you thought telling them about sex would be the hard discussion!

So what do you do? Do you tell or not tell? And to that I say . . . it's up to you. Hey, I'm not a damn child psychologist. I'm not going to take the rap for upsetting your kid, and I'm not going to send you lattes for the rest of your life in your new small town. Each family is different, each kid is different, and it's a very personal decision. I just know that after our daughter finds out the truth and the dust is settled, I'll be greatly relieved! Sure, it'll be the end of an era filled with magic and enchantment, but I'll finally be able to get the thank-you hugs for all the great gifts I scurry around town to get, so I say, screw it!

Claus-trophobia

As any parent knows, children are a fearful lot. And since all kids are different, so are their fears. Some are afraid of dogs. Others of long-legged spiders. And some are so timid, they're scared of the cursive letter M at the end of the Zaboomafu logo and go screaming out of the room whenever the show is on (please don't tell me my kid's the only one who does that). But no matter what fears your child may have, there's an excellent chance that he's afraid of Santa Claus. Although there are many children who race to see Santa, there are many others that run the other way.

And who can blame them, really? Santa's an imposing figure with beady eyes, no fashion sense, and hair reminiscent of Nick Nolte in his infamous mug shot. Plus, he wants to have kids sit on his lap like that icky guy at the park that Mommy always keeps clear of. But what really evokes panic in these two-foot irrational toddlers is that, unlike the guy at the park, Mommy's more than happy to hand him her precious little baby. She doesn't even give a crap that they cry enough tears to refresh a potted plant. Instead of running over to save them, she just stands there with a stupid smile on her face like the one she gives Daddy when he offers to give her a few hours of alone time.

If your child reacts like this during his first visit with Santa, chances are he's been traumatized enough to develop the all too common condition of coulrophobia. Once coulrophobia sets in, it sets in hard and can take years to erode. Until then, you must steer clear of the circus, street performers, theme parks, and all birthday parties with costumed characters.

Coulrophobia is as prevalent in children as their nasty desire to eat sand. If you don't believe me, just log on to youtube.com and check out other tiny tots who scream for dear life whenever Santa is near. In most cases, children do outgrow this condition, just as they do their need to eat sand, but until then, it's best to avoid him—and that park with the cats who use the sandbox as their own personal toilet.

If this is the first year you're going to introduce your child to Kris Kringle, take his lead. If, as you approach the big guy, your kid starts to tremble and the tears start to flow, *back away*! Forcing Santa on your child won't work any better than when your mom tried to force those "nice guys with the good personalities" on you when you were dating. At this tender young age, forcing the issue will only lead to avoiding all birthday parties that have costumed characters like Cinderella and the Power Rangers. And if it's a drop-off party where you can have an hour to yourself to get a quick mani-pedi, that'll be one hell of a price to pay. Like anything else when it comes to your kid, use baby steps.

"I took the day off work and took my daughter to Disneyland midweek so it'd be less crowded. After about twenty minutes and $100 in tickets, Alice in Wonderland walked by and smiled at my daughter. She was so inconsolable we had to leave the park."

—Jane

So when you and your child are near Santa, take your kid's lead, and never push the issue. If you're lucky, you may have given birth to a kid that's actually immune to coulrophobia, and you can have a lifetime of fond Santa memories, great holiday photos, and years of beautifully painted nails.

The High Cost of Frame

Anyone that's bought a picture of their kid sitting on Santa's lap knows that it doesn't come cheap! I'm not sure what kind of lifestyle Santa has to maintain in his off-season, but it must be full of expensive trinkets for keeping the Mrs. happy in that frozen wasteland with no Starbucks or Forever 21 in sight. If you've ever had to spring for the complete portrait packet with accompanying CD and DVD, you know just what I mean.

Santa has a good deal going on. I haven't seen this kind of price gouging since they started selling bottled water. Things were different a decade ago when Santa's cameras used film and the portraits had to be mailed. But now with digital technology, there are no hard costs for film or postage. The price of a sheet of photo paper, a blank CD and DVD is mere pennies as well. Since a photo shoot with Santa can easily cost $15 for one freakin' 5x6, $10 extra for a CD, and $30 for a DVD, we're talking about a 500% profit margin!

I know many of you are mad as hell and don't want to pay it any more. You pass on the deluxe package and bring a camera of your own. Sure you feel like a tightwad. It's like bringing popcorn to the movies. And like the popcorn, you don't get the same results. With the popcorn, it's not warm and ladled with artery-clogging buttery-flavored oil. With the photo, the elves don't try as hard to get your kid to look in the right direction and smile pretty for the camera, since you have no right to complain if the picture sucks.

Getting a photo of your kid with Santa is not only financially frustrating, but it's also mentally exhausting. It starts at home when you force your kid into his itchy seasonal garb while he fights and screams. Then it's off to the mall where you wait in a line that's longer than the one at any Harry Potter premier. By the time your kid gets to the front, he's old enough to grow underarm hair. When it's finally your turn, you hand your kid over to his nemesis, and both of you endure a dizzying array of bells and whistles to distract your kid long enough to stop the crying. In the end, you're both traumatized and in desperate need of a bottle. Yours of course, being from the nearby Liquor Barn.

In the end, after all the time, trouble, effort, and money, you have a photo to treasure throughout the years. It's a glossy 8x10 of your adorable offspring in the arms of Santa, tearstained, and tugging at his itchy collar. Every time you look at it you get a warm, fuzzy feeling in your heart, or perhaps a tingling sensation in your left arm, as the stress returns like holiday posttraumatic stress disorder.

"I was going to outsmart Santa by buying a cheap picture and then scanning it into my home scanner and printing out a whole bunch of them, but there was no such thing as a cheap picture."

—Greg

If you don't want to spend the money, or go though the hassle of getting a photo of your kid with Santa, turn to technology. Go to your local computer store and spring for the program called Photoshop. Then you can cut your child's happy head from his past birthday party, and paste it next to Santa. No fuss. No muss. And no tingly sensation! Sounds like the perfect solution for all!

Stop the InSanta-ty

Here's a problem. You've gone to the toy store and pushed and shoved and threatened your way to the last Torture Me Elmo doll in your entire state because it was the one and only thing that your sweet baby boy wanted this Christmas. But when you take your kid to the mall and he climbs on board Santa's lap, he tells Santa that, "The only thing I want this year is a green Ninja action fighter." Man, are you screwed.

Or, you and your spouse agree to keep to a strict budget this year so as not to reenact the "dipping into the IRA account despite the enormous penalties" horror of the past. But when Santa asks your kid what she wants, she rattles off a list longer than the Ken Starr report. No way can you afford all that crap, let alone remember what the heck she even said. Again, completely screwed.

Or let's try this one on for giggles: Your daughter tells Santa, "The only thing that'll make me happy this Christmas is if you give me a magic ballerina outfit exactly like the one I saw on Nickelodeon like two summers ago." Screwed, screwed, screwed.

Yes, it seems that a visit with Santa can throw a wrench in your gift-giving plans that's bigger than any found in a Craftsman tool set. You thought you had it covered two weeks ago when you sat your kid down and helped her write a letter to Santa that listed everything in detail that she could possibly want. But as any parent who's had to buy a Cinderella, Dorothy, butterfly, *and* fairy princess costume for one Halloween season knows, kids tend to change their minds a lot!

Having trouble with Christmas presents doesn't get any easier as your child grows older. My daughter is at that dangerous age where she's young enough to believe in Santa, but old enough to navigate her way through cyberspace. This year, the only things she wants Santa to bring is a retired collectable Webkinz stuffed cheeky-dog that she found on eBay. Price tag: $1,800. She's convinced that since she's been good all year, Santa will get her whatever she wants. Those were the rules laid out so many years ago and those are the rules she's sticking with. It was fine years ago when all she wanted was a Polly Pocket doll, but an $1,800 stuffed animal? It seems you're not the only one that's screwed.

So what's a parent to do to keep child and budget on track with gifts? How can you brainwash your kid to pick an affordable toy that's easy to find and stick with it? I'll be honest. You'd have a better chance of stopping those annoying penile enhancement e-mails than achieve this goal. My best suggestions is that before your set your kid down on

Santa's lap, whisper in Santa's ear what gift you already got her so he can say something like, "So, Sarah, I'm sure a wonderful girl like yourself would enjoy an Easy Bake Oven with assorted cake and cookie mixes." Then, before your kid can answer, pull her off Santa like a giant tick. Since Santa's caused you so much stress during the holidays, it's the very least he could do.

Christmas Envy

As much of a pain in the ass it is to deal with Santa, not dealing with him can be even worse. If you have children and celebrate Chanukah, Kwanzaa, or any other religious holiday that falls in the month of December, you know exactly what I mean. It's as if the whole world is in New Orleans celebrating Mardi Gras, and you're stuck in Buffalo getting a boil lanced.

Your young children will turn green with envy when they go next door to play with little Billy and discover that his house has transformed into a magical paradise. "How come Billy gets to have a real live tree in his house?" "How come Billy gets a stack of presents to open?" "How come Billy has a kitchen full of treats when all we have is organic health snacks that taste like lawn?" All this month it's Billy, Billy, Billy! Damn that Billy!

It's hard for small children to not feel left out. And it's hard for teenagers not to either. It doesn't seem fair that their friends come back from Christmas vacation with sparkly new iPods and lots of new clothes. It's not right that their friends got to visit their cousins in Hollywood when the most exotic place they went during vacation was Ikea.

It's not fair, Mom, it's just not fair! (Sound effect: stomping feet and bedroom door slam!)

Granted, society tries to even things out. They put a giant menorah in the shopping mall, and sometimes a Happy Kwanzaa sign as well. But it really doesn't do much good. It's like taking baby aspirin to kill labor pains, or throwing a few African Americans into soap operas to appease the NAACP. No matter where kids look, they're assaulted by festive Christmas décor. "Can we become a Christian too, Mommy? Huh? Can we, pleeeezze?" "No sweetie, our religion doesn't believe that Jesus Christ was the son of God." "Awww, crap, Ma! Can't we just believe in December when there's so much cool stuff at the Apple store?"

You tell your kid there are some great things about being _____(insert your religion here). If you're Jewish, you can push the whole eight-gift thing during Chanukah. So what if they're ceremoniously small, like a handful of erasers or a bag of tube socks. You know as the words come out of your mouth, there's not a chance in hell you're going to win this battle.

Ironically, Christmas envy works the opposite way for adults. Every December as they suffer through the enormous stress and madness that surrounds Christmas, they're jealous of their non-Christian friends who breeze through the holidays without cracking open a checkbook. There have no massive shopping to do, no elaborate feasts to plan, no exorbitant shipping costs, no visiting in-laws or divorce-inspiring arguments with their mates. And come December 26, they don't fall over in a heaping pile of exhaustion.

For whatever reason, unbridled commercialism hasn't infiltrated into religious celebrations in the Jewish, Hindu, or Muslim faiths. Perhaps if we mix and mingle all the religious holidays together, then every faith around the world will become stressful, the entire population will become broke, and mankind will finally be equal! Halleluiah! On that note, let's mix things up and remake some of the most cherished holiday classics so that they're more user friendly to all religions:

- It's a Wonderful Life, You Putz
- Rashid, the Red Nosed Reindeer
- Miracle on Karumwa Street
- Deck the Halls with Boughs of Challah
- Come, They Told Me, oh Ram-a-dam-dam
- Joy to the Moyl
- I'm Dreaming of a White Kwanzaa
- I'll Be Home for Latkes

Satan Claus

People never fail to surprise me. They say and do things so foreign to what I could ever imagine doing. They yell at the poor barista for putting 2 percent milk in their latte instead of 1 percent. They tell horrible labor stories to pregnant women. And they set you up on a blind date with a guy that looks just like your dad (some things I'll never forget).

But sometimes their beliefs span past our world and travel into the world of the occult. I'm not talking about people who believe in things like ghosts and ESP. I'm not even talking about those who think it's possible to bend spoons with the power of thought. I'm talking about the ones that truly believe that Santa is an evil, threatening symbol that's somehow connected with the devil. Do they think this because of some religious myth or because they both dress in red? No. They believe this to be true because the letters in the word "Santa" are the same as ones that are used in the word "Satan." Unbelievable, huh?

At first I thought that was the silliest thing I'd ever heard. Just because both words happen to have the same letters does not make them equal. But then, like any responsible author, I shunned my personal beliefs and did some research on the subject. Startling enough, I couldn't get past the many other anagrams that defied all logic and reason. Here are some that I encountered:

- Mother-in-law: woman Hitler
- Elvis: lives
- Slot machines: cash lost in 'em
- Debit card: bad credit
- David Letterman: nerd amid late TV
- Statue of Liberty: built to stay free
- Snooze alarm: alas, no more Zs!
- Mel Gibson: bong smile

As you can see, perhaps there is something to this mysterious connection after all! Even if you don't believe, perhaps you can use this excuse to get out of dealing with Santa Claus this year. Just tell your spouse that you won't be taking the kids to see Santa this year because of your new spiritual beliefs. Then *he'll* be the one to finally deal with the traffic, the parking, and the long lines, while you relax at home eating ice cream from the container and watching "Plastic Surgery: Before and After"! Hey, maybe there's some logic to this whole occult thing after all!

Chapter 4

the twelve days of
christmas parties

If the holidays are a time of anything, they're a time when people gather around with friends and loved ones to celebrate the birth of our Savior and sing his praises. What? They don't? Oh yeah. They gather around to guzzle spiked eggnog, eat fattening meals, and make out with any drunken fool that crosses their path. Ah, what a tribute to God's only son! Yes, if Christmas is anything, it's a time to eat, drink, and be merry. Or shall I say, overeat, overdrink, and be so merry that nine months later you give your child a half sibling. Many people are inherently weak and look for any opportunity to overindulge, and all the parties that surround the holiday season give them plenty of opportunity.

On an individual basis, parties can be great fun. You get all dolled up in your festive attire and don't have to spend another night watching reruns or Christmas specials hosted by Al Roker. But when you add up all the parties together, it's just a whirlwind of stress in an already stress-filled month. And as we all know after helping ourselves to thirds of Thanksgiving dinner, too much of a good thing really isn't all that good. And Christmas parties are no exception to this rule.

During the three weeks before Christmas, there are ample parties to go to. Sure, there's the coveted Saturday night soiree, (it's the June wedding of the holiday party circuit), but there are plenty of others that fall during the week. Your calendar is full, not only with the actual parties, but with all the other crap surrounding the party, like buying the hostess gifts, getting new party clothes, fighting the traffic to get to the party and the traffic coming home, stopping off at the ATM to get cash to pay the sitter, making your husband drive the sitter home, and then nursing your hangover the following day! Yes, your calendar is chock full all right!

Like most other things in life, and most other chapters in this book, there are plenty of lessons to be learned. There are pointers to give, stories to relay, and jokes to be told. So let's get down to business and learn the good, the bad, and the ugly side of Christmas parties.

Office Parties

It cracks me up that for 364 days of the year (minus weekends and holidays if you want to get picky) people dress up in their pinstriped suits and appropriate shoes, and comply with office protocol. They work in cubicles, obey their bosses, and are careful not to brush alongside a coworker for fear of being slapped with a sexual harassment suit. But, during a company's annual holiday office party, all bets are off (as are some of the clothes), and the average Joe Schmo parties harder than Nicole Ritchie before she got knocked up.

During the typical holiday bash, office behavior goes out the door, and employees feel comfortable doing things that'd they'd never think of doing otherwise. Liquor gets consumed, voices get raised, and body parts get Xeroxed. Supervisors have the liquid courage to tell laypersons they find them attractive. Employees have the strength to demand a hefty raise. Not only is office protocol abandoned during the holiday bash, so is office attire. Ties are removed, up-do's are taken down, blouses are unbuttoned to show off cleavage, and constricting clothing such as high shoes and pantyhose are tossed aside. The once dignified and professional office is transformed into what could easily be mistaken for the set of *Animal House*.

Who you bring with you to your office party is critical. Office parties are not the place for arm candy or first dates since *you'll* be the one that's judged when your date dances topless on the table or eats the caviar by the spoonful. If you're married, office parties can be a yearly source of contention. If the spouses aren't invited, the one left behind is resentful, wondering what their significant other is doing. And, if they are allowed to come, they feel uncomfortable watching their partner laugh at inside jokes with pretty associates or ruggedly good-looking coworkers. Like high school reunions, office parties are always a lose-lose situation for spouses.

If you work for a big corporation, your party may not be as fun as those of smaller companies. The larger the corporation, the more legalities must be followed. For instance, it can't be called a Christmas party for fear of upsetting non-Christians. It has to serve alcohol-free beverages so as not to upset the alcoholics. There must be nonmeat options so as not to offend vegetarians and organic choices for those with an aversion to pesticides. And it has to be held after dark so as not to upset those whose religion forbids them from partying during daylight hours. These days it's all about being politically correct so as not to be sued. While this does make for less hurt feelings, it also makes for a party as exciting as watching someone's arm hair grow.

The day after the office party, the decorations are taken down and all decorum is restored. The buns return, as do the three-piece suits. Sure, there may be a few winks between staff members who raised the roof, or averted eye contact because of things that might have been done. But after a few days, memories fade, apologies are accepted, and embarrassing Xeroxes are destroyed—or posted on the Internet for further humiliation.

That being said, here are some basic guidelines to follow regarding office parties:

- Limit yourself to one cocktail. Order a drink you don't like so you're less likely to finish it, or stick with a sipping drink like scotch instead of a sweet one you'll guzzle down like Vitamin Water.
- Stick to benign conversations about nonpersonal topics. Office parties are not the place to discuss politics, religion, or if bigger really is better.
- Before you leave, thank the boss for a terrific party. If you have to go early, make up a good excuse.
- DON'T GO TO A SECONDARY LOCATION! Even if everyone else is moving to a nearby home or strip bar, do not go with them!

"Last year I got so drunk, I didn't remember much of the Christmas party except that I thought my boss's wife was good-looking. But the next day, my security pass didn't let me in the building and I realized I must have done something really, really bad."

—Matt

Tree-Trimming Parties

Whenever I get invited to a tree-trimming party, I have to laugh. To me, this kind of get-together is just a cheap ass lazy way of getting other people to buy you ornaments and decorate your tree. When you think about it, a tree-trimming party is like a Yuletide version of a barn raising. In both instances, you help perform some labor-intensive household ritual, and you're rewarded with refreshments, albeit stiff drinks are substituted for sun tea.

In theory, it sounds so enchanting. You and your friends, all huddled around a pine-scented tree and warmed by a crackling fire. Carols are sung and iced cookies are passed on a decorative plate. But in reality, things can go horribly awry if the hosts are control freaks and dictate specific ways their ornaments must be hung. The heirlooms must be grouped together to adhere to a schematic theme. The breakables must go above a certain branch level if there are children or pets in the home. And the colored balls must follow a universal placement to avoid obvious gaps. As you hang the porcelain Lladro "Baby's first Christmas," you pray that the limb you're using is strong enough to support it. Or you reach for your eggnog and inadvertently knock off a crystal snowflake and your heart stops as you await that horrible "crash" sound on the hardwood floor. The whole thing's more stressful than waiting for your STD test results (and you should all know what that feels like since it's the responsible thing to do. End of speech).

Let's face it. A tree-trimming party isn't fun for anyone, except of course the hosts who get you to do all their work for them. In fact, a party like this is just a heartbeat away from a "C'mon over to my house and help prep my tax audit!" When invited to a tree-trimming party, I don't actually *want* to go, but somehow, I always do, because, let's face it, it's always easier to do other people's crappy chores than your own (just wash someone else's dishes and you'll see), and, did I mention there are iced cookies?

If you *are* a fan of tree-trimming parties, here are some other occasions that you might be interested in attending as well:

"You're invited to my house to ...
- spread steer manure over my newly seeded lawn."
- pretreat the skid marks on my husband's underwear."
- remove the gizzards from the raw chicken I'm cooking tonight."
- fold my fitted sheets."
- clean out all the fuzzy things from the back of my produce drawer."
- pop the zits on my teenager's back."
- express my dog's anal gland."

It'll be quite the good time!

Caroling Parties

Every year, my friend Jennifer invites us over for a caroling party. And every year, I dread it. It's not that Jennifer doesn't throw a good party. She does. She invites some interesting people, makes her home festive and cozy, and serves up a warm crab dip that Emeril Lagasse would die for. It's just that whenever you mix grownups drinking alcohol with kids consuming sugar, the results are never pretty. Invariably the grownups turn into kids, and the kids turn into wild animals. They knock into each other, slam the doors, and tease each other unmercifully—and I'm talking about the adults (ba-dum-dum). Then, after everyone is properly inebriated and has a good sugar high going, it's time to hit the streets and bring all the craziness outside.

The true fun begins as you try to get your kids ready. Since I live in Southern California, there is no cold weather to dress for. Our stress is getting our kids back in their flipflops and making them carry a water bottle to ward off dehydration. But if you do live where it's cold, getting your kids rebundled to go outside is like getting toothpaste back in its tube. Coats have to be buckled, gloves must be put back on, and scarves need to be tied. Soon, your kid has more layers than a lasagna.

Once properly dressed, the next challenge is to find a neighbor to sing to. This isn't 1950, when homeowners would readily open their doors to anyone who rings their bell. Back then, husbands were home by five and the whole family would be gathered around the dinner table enjoying a nice pot roast supper. Nowadays, no one is home anymore. People work late and kids have soccer practice, and someone inevitably stops off at a fast food joint for a bucket of grub.

Besides, we've all seen enough evening news shows to know that opening your door without a firearm and pit bull is not a wise move.

But then it happens! A Christmas miracle far greater than a virgin being knocked up . . . someone actually opens their door! Yes, halleluiah, you've found the one person who doesn't watch the news, is unemployed, doesn't have kids, eats frozen dinners, and has TIVO to pause the exciting episode of *Deal or No Deal*! Quickly, the group starts singing "Jingle Bells," music fills the air, and the world is bathed in Christmas spirit. But afterward, there's an awkward silence as the homeowner stares at the group. Does he offer a tip? Shake everyone's hand? Pass out candy? (No, wrong holiday.) In the end, he simply says, "Merry Christmas" and goes back inside to see how much the banker is offering. By now you're freezing, your buzz has worn off, and your kid just puked crab dip all over your shoes!

Everyone heads back to the party to refuel on peppermint mojitos and fudge. In the end, everyone leaves feeling spent and swears to make up some excuse next year and skip the whole shebang. But the funny thing is, when the next year comes, all the same people seem to be there. I guess despite the cold, the crazy kids, and the fact that you only found one person at home, a caroling party isn't so bad after all. Perhaps that one round of "Jingle Bells" warmed everyone's heart just enough to make them want to do it again. Or perhaps it was that incredible dip. I guess we'll never know.

Cookie Swap Parties

Granted, even I, the queen of cynicism, am hard pressed to find much fault behind the idea of a cookie swap party. I mean, is there anything more perfect in life than a buttery piece of disk-shaped perfection? It makes my mouth water and my heart sing. It conveys all that is good and pure and right in this world in just a few bites. But even with this heavenly piece of confection, there are some inherent faults with the "party" aspect of the cookie party experience.

Before I delve into these faults, I want to take a minute, and a paragraph, to explain what a cookie swap party is for those that are unaware. A cookie swap party (also known as a cookie exchange) is a tradition that started decades ago where a hostess invites several women over, asking each one to bring a dozen of one kind of cookie for each guest. Today's version is relatively unchanged. If, for example, you're invited to a party with ten other guests, you must bring ten dozen of the same kind of cookie. Once at the party, you give a dozen cookies to each guest, and receive a dozen cookies from each one in return. In sum, you bring 120 similar cookies with you, and you leave with 120 of a variety of cookies made by others. Are we all clear? Good.

"I spent hours making my favorite cookies, but I had to trade them in for horrible ones. One kind looked like oatmeal hockey pucks, another smelled like perfume, and the rest I'm sure were store bought. I felt robbed. I need to become friends with a better circle of bakers."

—Allison

Now that we know what a cookie swap party is, let's be clear on what some of its faults can be:

You may get stuck with some truly crappy cookies. Sure you leave with an assortment of cookies instead of all of one kind, but there are always some loser cookies in the bunch, like the candied fruit lavender surprise or the ones with nuts you hate, or the dried-out cookies that the baker claims to be biscotti but you know are only called this to cover for the fact that they were overcooked.

You're stuck with 120 cookies. What the hell are you going to do with all of them? If you had kept the ones you made, at least you could give them out as gifts. But you feel awkward dolling out other people's work and passing it off as your own. And if you cop to the truth and tell people you didn't make them, the gift has a tacky, regifting quality.

If you have a weight issue—in other words, if you're a human being living on planet Earth—how can you possibly resist eating 120 cookies when they're just sitting there looking at you?

Time is at a premium during the busy holidays, and between the family dinners, the school parties, the hungry kids, and the visiting relatives, you're already a full-time cook. You're hard pressed to find time to nuke a frozen meal, let alone bake ten dozen cookies (okay, eleven dozen since we all know you're going to eat an extra dozen's worth in dough).

I know there's great tradition and history surrounding the cookie swap party. I'm sure generations ago ladies looked forward to baking their prized cookies and getting together with the womenfolk to exchange them. Not only because they got to try a variety of cookies they never would've been able to otherwise, but also because going to these parties got them out of doing their daily chores of sweeping dirt floors and cleaning the outhouse. But now there's a bakery in every supermarket that offers plastic containers brimming with any variety of cookie imaginable. My guess is that a cookie swap party is pretty obsolete, and if it were to disappear, it wouldn't be missed much. Kind of like your appendix, or *The View*. But as long as there are unpleasant chores for women to do, I imagine a cookie swap party will live on.

The Holiday Spread

Forget the fact that Christmas parties can be stressful, embarrassing, career ending, boring, or exhausting. The biggest assault of the holiday bash is that it can make you fat. Yes, people, F-A-T. It seems the biggest spread of the holiday season actually takes place on your ass. According to some studies, the average person gains seven pounds during the holiday season spanning from Thanksgiving to New Year's Day. Personally, I consider myself a little above average, which is why I tend to gain at least ten.

Sure. Go ahead and shake your head in disbelief. Studies have been wrong before. We now know that being in cold weather doesn't give you a cold, or that reading in bad light doesn't ruin your eyes (check it out, it's true). But when you take a minute to think about all the food you consume during the holidays, like the heavy meals, the party hors d'oeuvres, the creamy alcoholic beverages, the chocolate Santas, the gingerbread men, and all the yummy samples at the supermarket, you start to realize just how many extra calories you actually eat.

With so many decadent treats, your willpower caves as easily as a shopoholic watching Marie Osmond on QVC. Once you take that first bite of holiday heaven, it's hard to stop. After all, Christmas comes but once a year, and the food is oh, so good. So you give yourself a holiday hall pass and order the festive eggnog latte instead of your usual decaf with skim. That'll be 500 extra calories please! You may as well have ordered a cup of ass fat.

Not only is there plenty to eat around the holidays, there's also plenty of reason to eat it. Stress abounds this time of year, and if you're the type of person who eats when you're stressed, watch out (if you're the type who relieves stress by chewing on pencils or, God forbid, by exercising, then just skip ahead— and never ever talk to me). People also overindulge because they're depressed or lonely or anxious. This time of year is all about emotional eating, which may explain why Christmas is all about treats. Think about it. There aren't a hell of a lot of snack options associated with Arbor Day. No vermin-themed lattes geared toward Groundhog's Day. But there are a boat-load of beauties and fattening items that surround this most wonderfully fattening time of the year. Here's a sampling:

Treat	Calories
Holiday dinner:	between 1,000 to 4,500
Starbucks eggnog latte:	510
Eggnog (spiked):	400
Hot chocolate:	300
Chocolate Santa:	200 to 400
Iced gingerbread man:	150

Right about now, I should come up with a paragraph of ingenious ways to prevent you from taking a walk on the wildly fattening side. A list of creative ideas to have you eat less during the holidays and maybe even shed a few pounds. While I'm at it, I might as well clue you in on how to get rid of wrinkles, make your husband pick up his own damn crap, and make a killing in the stock market. Man, I'm good!

But let's be honest. From Thanksgiving to New Year's, there'll be lots of great food around and lots of great reasons to eat it. We all know the only way not to gain any weight is to not put these fattening foods in our mouths. So, perhaps a good goal isn't to lose any weight during the holidays, but rather not to gain any. On that note, here are some suggestions for how to limit the amount of food you eat to avoid the holiday spread:

- Instead of using a dinner plate at the buffet, grab a smaller appetizer plate instead.
- Drink plenty of water while you're at the party to fill you up.
- Have a healthy snack before leaving your house so you're less likely to indulge. I know it sounds odd to eat before you go to a party, but you clean up before the housekeeper comes and you think that's normal behavior.
- Load your plate full of the healthier stuff and only put one no-no on your plate.
- Offer to bring something to the party and make it low-cal so you'll be assured that there's something healthy to eat.

- Don't stand near the food table. You're only human for God's sake, and who can resist the chestnut stuffing or bowl of red and green M&M's? Not I.
- Chew gum. My grandma would smack your hand if she saw you, but at least you won't be able to eat anything with a wad of gum in your mouth.
- If you're going to drink, only have one and use a generous amount of sugar-free tonic or bubbly water.

If you know ahead of time that you're going to go all out during the holidays and eat like there's no tomorrow, go on a diet the month before Christmas to lose some weight beforehand. Better yet, be a contestant on *Dancing with the Stars*. Those people always seem to lose like thirty pounds.

Ho Ho Haute Couture

You can't talk about holiday parties without talking about holiday fashion. And I don't mean the sleek Donna Karan number with the shiny beads and cashmere wrap. I'm talking about the all-out, elaborate holiday fashions that are so atrocious they make my eyeballs bleed when I look at them.

When it comes to holiday glamour don'ts, fashion victims tend to fall in two distinct categories. One is the dorky red-and-green sweatshirts adorned with three-dimensional reindeer antlers or embroidered Christmas tree with flashing lights (note to self: any piece of clothing that requires a battery pack is a definite no-no). Of course, as any fashion expert will tell you, it's all about the accessories, which is why this look is accented with small ornament earrings with tree hooks inserted right through the ear hole, and a Santa hat that, when the button is pressed, chimes out a festive rendition of "Joy to the World" (reread note to self).

The other wardrobe extreme is to turn your Christmas look into something R-rated. The dude version is to wear a shirt with a cartoon picture of Santa dry-humping Rudolf. For a woman, it's the clever mixing of a skintight shirt that reads "I've been very naughty this year" combined with a red felt miniskirt. Throw on some fishnet stockings and you're ready to ho-ho-ho it up all around town!

This fashion faux pas has grown by epic proportions over the last few years and is now even celebrated at "Ugly Christmas Outfit" parties all over the country. These shindigs are popping up everywhere, and guests are actually required to dress in their worst holiday sweaters or outfits. Then, prizes are awarded to the worst articles of clothing, whether it be singing elf shoes or Rudolf belt buckle with lighted red nose.

This holiday blunder is like a communicable disease and has spread to all members of the family. Even our pets! It's now commonplace to dress your dog in holiday attire (well, it's commonplace here in L.A. anyway). It's no surprise really, since people treat their bite-sized canines like kids. Specialty stores sell four-poster doggie beds, puppy strollers, and "baby" carriers so that dogs can be carted around on the owner's chest like an infant. A store near me even sells doggie playpens and puppy announcement cards! And of course, during the holidays, there's a full line of proper Christmas outfits including Mr. and Mrs. Claus costumes, reindeer antler hats, and elf attire.

The only exception I grant to these wardrobe malfunctions is the holiday look worn by babies. Babies, like runway models, look good in anything, even if it's covered in puke (babies and models have the puke thing in common as well).

No matter how much green and red frou-frou the outfit contains, you put it on your kid and you're bound to get "ooohs" and "awwws" from any audience.

So if you're going to a holiday bash, be respectful of other people's eyeballs and check yourself out in the mirror before you leave. If you're wearing anything themed, obscene, or battery packed, change clothes immediately or go to a party that actually celebrates this look! If not, you'll run the risk of being blackmailed by holiday photos, or worse, being electrocuted when your beer spills on your battery pack. Remember, drinking and juvenile holiday attire just doesn't mix.

gifts: it's the thought that counts (good one, huh?)

What started out as a few presents from the three Wise Men has grown by epic proportions. Those thoughtful trinkets of frankincense and myrrh have evolved into budget-breaking plasma TVs, state-of-the-art Xboxes, and expensive cars complete with oversized bows tied to the rooftops. In fact, if you're not financing a gift, or paying for it in three easy payments, it doesn't even count as a proper gift.

These days, we're not only expected to exchange gifts with good friends and family, we're also expected to exchange them with coworkers, neighbors, and every acquaintance we've met since *Different Strokes* ruled the airwaves. It's a desperate race to decide on the gifts, track them down, and scramble to get them delivered before the big day! It's enough to make even Ben Stein show emotion!

Your head is full of questions. "What should I buy?" "How much should I spend?" "Whom should I buy for?" (Actually,

you'll say "who" since no one uses proper grammar anymore.)
Your energy level's high and inventory's getting low. It's enough
to make you want to forget about Christmas and spend the day
in bed. In hopes of bringing your stress level down and your
enjoyment level up, let's see what we can do to ease the pain.

The Impersonal Touch

In these material days, it's not what you get, it's how much
it costs. The only thought behind a gift anymore is deciding
which credit card to use to pay for it. Gifts with meaning are
so last century. In fact, for the entire month of December, I
urge you not to watch a repeat of *Little House on the Prairie* or
you'll be ashamed of how homogenized and thoughtless gift
giving has truly become. Back in those hard days, without
flattening irons or Viking stoves, gifts actually meant something. There were no reindeer Chia pets to buy for every
Tom, Dick, or Jebediah that crossed your path. Instead, Half
Pint sold her hair to buy Ma some fabric. Pa tended a neighbor's fields to get Manly some tobacco. Sure, they had stupid
names, but they had generous hearts, and that's what Christmas was really about.

Now those days are gone, and there's rarely any thought
behind a gift. With so many people to buy for, gift giving
has turned into a "let's just get this over with as quickly
as possible" kind of thing. It's a bikini wax with attached
gift card. Now, we're grateful if someone took the time to
log on to the Internet to point and click their way to a nice
gift. And if they spent the extra time and money to have it
wrapped and enclosed a computerized greeting card, it must
be love!

Yes, shopping on the Internet can be impersonal, but it's one step above the popular gift card, which makes sense to everyone except the recipient. The stores are thrilled because, in most cases, the recipient buys more than the gift card is worth, gets something for less and never redeems the remainder, loses the card, or waits so long to use it, it reduces value or even expires. Not only are the stores happy, but the gift giver is happy too. Gift cards are readily available (you can often get them at the supermarket) and with almost no effort, people get to scratch one more person off their shopping list.

Look, I don't mean to be so harsh. I know how long your list is and that you got carpal tunnel just writing the damn thing. And you don't even know half the people on it! But if you *do* know the person, take a minute to make your gift personal. Think about their hobbies, their collections, and their taste. Instead of a gift card, buy a gift that symbolizes an event you shared together or a reminder of a special time. Or buy something and have their name put on it. Even a turd would look better if it were engraved. Okay. Maybe not.

If you have a photo of the recipient on your computer, you're all set to go (if not, have one scanned and put on a disk). There's a bevy of personal items you can create from one photo, such as a deck of cards, a coffee mug, stationary, clothing, or even a postage stamp (see resource section for specific Web sites). If you have several photos, make a calendar, a photo book, or some coasters. Or, do what my friend Brandi did and make homemade wine charms. She printed photos out on special shrinky-dink paper she got at a craft store, shrunk them down to size, and then stuck a hoop earring through each one!

There are great Web sites that specialize in personal items too. Instead of giving some store-bought treats, go to *www.chipndough.com* where you not only get great cookies, but you can also download a photo that's duplicated on the cookie tin cover. Instead of a generic book for their kid, log onto *www.flattenme.com* and create one where the character has the kid's face and name. Another great site is *www.americanpersonalizedproducts.com* where you can find dozens of personal items to choose from.

As you can see, it doesn't take much time to turn a gift into a treasured keepsake. With a little thought, and perhaps a few clicks of the mouse, (or a trip to the craft store if you're going to make those great wine charms), you can give a gift you're proud of. One that says, "I thought of you" instead of "Here, I had to get you something so take it already."

A Gift That's Taken Too Personally

When it comes to personal gifts, none is as important as the one you give your significant other. Not because it symbolizes how much you love that person, but because if you muck it up, it'll be held against you for many years to come.

"I had no idea what to get my wife so I bought her a bread warmer so the bread would stay hot at the dinner table. It's been over fifteen years now, and she still brings it up every Christmas."

—Art

The reason there are so many pitfalls to fall into is that men and women think differently when it comes to gift giving. Men tend to have bad listening skills, which explains the fact that you hint for a Barefoot Contessa cookbook, but wind up with some slippers. Men also have as much knowledge of women's dress sizes as they do about women's anatomy, which explains why they never buy anything that fits, and why they get so aroused by the word "uvula."

Women, on the other hand, read too much into a gift. When choosing a gift for their mate, they lament for days deciding on the perfect one, then discuss it at length with each of their girlfriends, search high and low for the exact one, and expect their guy to think it's the best thing since the NFL package (which is what they really want). When they receive a gift from their mate, they dissect its every meaning. Did he give me a new coffee pot because he hates my coffee? Did he give me the day at the spa because he wants me to go away for a while? The possibilities are endless.

In the gift-giving pyramid, presents to our significant other are at the top of the pressure filled heap, especially at the beginning of the relationship when a wrong gift can actually end the relationship. But after years of being together and so many disappointing presents, gift giving evolves into something truly comforting. Women, frustrated by getting so many loser gifts, end up buying themselves what they like and writing his name on the gift. And men have learned to just open their gift, pretend that they love it, then toss it aside, knowing that, after all these years, their significant other won't really give a crap anymore. Only after that level of a relationship is achieved can a couple really live happily ever after.

Loser Gifts

Sometimes you open a gift and a great big smile appears on your face without any effort whatsoever. Either the gift is something you've always wanted, or something you never even knew you wanted but now can't possibly live without—like those heavenly heated mattress pads. When this happens, savor every moment, people, because they're as rare as finding a Baldwin brother without a criminal record. With few exceptions, gifts inherently suck.

When you get a loser gift, it can be incredibly awkward, since you really only have one recourse: fake it. Force the sides of your mouth to form a smile, give the person a genuine-feeling hug, and say, "Wow, I just love it!" Sure, it'll take the acting skills of Anthony Hopkins, but if you fake it well, and the gift giver is anything like my husband, he won't have a clue.

Still, the question remains, why do so many gifts suck? To that, I'll propose some possible answers:

- People tend to buy gifts for others that they really want for themselves. Who cares if Aunt Maureen doesn't cook? You've always wanted a heart-shaped waffle iron, so darn it to donuts, that's what she's gonna get!
- People choose a gift because there's a little something in it for them. Everyone loves a free gift, including multimillion-dollar celebrities who clamor over Oscar baskets as if they were wedding dresses at Filene's Basement Once-a-Year sale. That's why, if Lancôme is giving away a "Dusty Rose" lipstick with every

twenty-dollar purchase, you can bet you'll be wearing "Dusty Rose" come this holiday season.

- People buy whatever's on sale. Sometimes there's a sale so incredible, you just can't resist it. Sure, your friend doesn't play golf and will never use a putting game, but he enjoys a green lawn so that's close enough.
- People have so many gifts to buy, and know so little about many of the people they're giving gifts to, they just grab something generic and hope for the best.

When you get a loser gift, you can forgive the gift giver if it's someone you hardly know. For instance, if the corporate office sends you a membership to the cheese-of-the-month club, you don't hold it against them for not knowing you're lactose intolerant. But if your husband gives it to you, you'll make him pay all right—by eating a big wedge of Gouda right before bedtime!

While it's true that one man's trash is another man's treasure, on the whole, there are gifts that are unquestionably trash to every man. On that note, here is my top-ten list of crappy presents that I hope to never get, and I promise to never give:

1. A generic gift basket. At first glance it can appear deceivingly delicious. But once you tear into it, it's basically stale crackers, some low-end cheese, and a handful of hard candies piled high on a butt load of shredded paper.

2. Fruitcake. Need I say more? Unless the recipient needs to bludgeon someone, just walk away.

3. Clothes. Once you're over the age of four, you like to pick out your own outfits. It's rare to get a piece of clothing that's in your taste, your size, and your color.

4. Artwork. If you don't like it, you'll have no choice but to hang it on the wall and stare at it every day in case the gift giver (code name for your mother-in-law) drops by without any warning.

5. Jewelry (see item #4). Although not as pressure-filled as artwork, you still have to wear it on occasion if you know the gift giver will be around.

6. Perfume. Unless it's a brand you know someone wears, don't tread those waters. People are very particular about how they smell.

7. Cleaning products. Especially when given by your husband or his mother.

8. Personal improvement items such as exercise products or nose hair clippers. Items such as these are basically saying, "You're fat and have nostril hair I can French braid."

9. Lingerie. Every year my husband gets me slutty lingerie and it's no secret who this gift is really meant to please.

10. Anything you can't return for cash.

If these are my list of no-no's, what, pray tell, are some of my yes-yeses? Good question. While not everyone likes the same things, here are some of my suggestions that should please some of the people most of the time:

1. Nice bath soaps and salts. These can be so expensive, people don't usually splurge on themselves.

2. Scented candles. While there *are* many brands that aren't very expensive, the beautifully smelling, elegantly packaged, imported kinds can easily run $40 and up.

3. Gadgets for men. Anything with a microchip, a video monitor, or rechargeable batteries seem to make guys go ga-ga.

4. Gourmet food. Who can resist imported goodies like Belgian chocolates or Omaha steaks? Many people can because they're about as expensive as flying to those places and buying them yourself.

5. Magazine subscriptions. Even if you only know a little bit about someone, there's a magazine to fit any interest.

6. Anything coated in chocolate—but maybe that's just me.

7. Anything that you can return for cash.

Uncharitable Contributions

There are times when making a donation in someone's name is an appropriate gift. I went to a wedding not long ago where the bride was a breast cancer survivor. In lieu of the standard sampling of Jordan Almonds, there was a card at each table setting stating that a donation was made in each guest's honor to a breast cancer charity. Although I really do enjoy those candy-coated treats, I found this to be a lovely gesture. But as much as there are many fine and deserving charities, I don't think that making a donation in someone's name is always the best practice during the holidays.

True, Christmas is unarguably the perfect time to think of others less fortunate than ourselves. And we should give as much as we can during this time. But, let's face it, a gift isn't a gift unless it's wrapped up in shiny paper with an impossible-to-open bow. There's a certain mystery about a gift. It's a box of endless possibilities. It doesn't matter if you're poor, middle class, or wealthy, there's a certain thrill about opening a gift that's never equaled by reading a piece of paper. It's like being offered a surprise dessert, only to be handed a nice piece of fruit.

As much as this situation can suck when it's made between friends and family, it sucks even more when it's made by your boss. If you're lucky enough to work for a company that believes in things like full health care, a matching 401K plan, and cake on everyone's birthday instead of just one for all the birthdays in that month, you probably count on a generous holiday bonus. Not so much to pay for a family vacation, but to pay for Christmas itself. You'll find that one of life's greatest mysteries, in addition to the one where you add up your age and divide it by a certain number and you'll always get nine, is that the amount of your Christmas bonus will always equal the amount of money you spend on the holidays. Just figure it out and see. Weird, huh?

But when it's Christmastime, and instead of a healthy bonus you're told the company made a charitable donation in your name, you're in deep holiday doo-doo. You needed that bonus to pay for next month's Visa bill! You worked your ass off this year, and all you have to show for it is a donation to Tree People (a very deserving organization by the way). And you don't even get the damn tax write off! Merry effin' Christmas to you, too!

It doesn't stop at Christmas, either. Donating money in someone else's name is the gift that keeps on giving. Throughout the next year you'll get dozens of calls from that charity asking for future contributions. If you say you can't afford to give, they'll send you a packet of requests to distribute to your neighbors. They'll call during dinner. They'll call during sex. Or even worse, they'll call during *Sex and the City* (sure it's a repeat, but that show really holds up)!

I know people really do have the best of intentions when they make a donation in someone else's name. But when it comes to giving money to a specific charity, I want to be the one who decides where my money should go. I want to decide how generous to be. I want to feel good about doing unto others. And I want that damn tax writeoff!

If you still feel that giving a donation in someone's name is a good idea, I have a compromise. Why not give to a charity where the recipient can decide where the funds should go, such as the following:

donorschoose.org: This charity gives much-needed funds to public schools in all 50 states. The recipient can decide to use the money for plenty of causes from school supplies to language fluency to field trips.

Changingthepresent.com: This charity offers a wide range of worldwide needy causes from disaster relief to saving an elephant to vaccinating a child.

Markmakers.org: This is a great one since it gets your kid involved. Someone makes a donation in your name and your child can pick from more than forty worldwide causes that involve helping children and the earth.

I'm not saying that people shouldn't give. That's what Christmas really is about, giving unto others. There's no better way to show you care than helping others in need, and no better time to do it. All I'm saying is that, unless you're sure a charitable donation to a specific charity is something the recipient would enjoy, think twice. And remember, if you do decide to donate, be smart. The holidays are a great time for fraud, and with over a million charities to choose from, you need to be careful. Never give out information over the phone or the Internet unless you contacted them. Legitimate charities will always provide information in writing and will never demand you give back account, credit card, or personal information. The holidays are expensive enough without getting ripped off.

How Rude!

Just when you thought you had a gift for everyone on your holiday list, there's an unexpected knock on your door that can only mean one thing: someone's coming over to bring you a present! Please, please, please don't let it be someone that wasn't on your list! But deep down you know it is. It always is. In this case, it's your daughter's classmate's mom, who's holding two perfectly wrapped presents, one for you and one for your daughter. How freakin' thoughtful! Now you're forced to open her gifts and have absolutely nothing to give in return. You suck.

Although you feel like a total loser, put things in perspective. You did nothing wrong. It's not your fault that this woman you hardly know, whose only connection to you is that she had sex around the same time you did to produce a child your kid's age, would come over without invitation and give you some presents. Screw her! In fact, if you think about it, it's downright selfish of her to put you in this spot in the first place! How dare she? She can take her little gifties and put them where the sun don't shine!

Another bad, bad scenario is when you and a friend agree to exchange gifts, but things don't play out as you expect. You and your friend are on equal playing fields in the gift-exchange game, meaning that she isn't your boss, isn't incredibly wealthy, or doesn't need your kidney. Equal playing fields means equal playing fields. But when you open your gift, you find that she gave you a gorgeous cashmere pashmina without any apparent stains or holes to significantly decrease its value. Holy crap! She gave you an amazing gift and all you got her was a nice bag of mulling spices! You suck again!

That's why when it comes to holiday gift giving, it's best to channel your inner girl scout and always be prepared. Keep a stash of extra gifts in varying degrees of value, from nice guest soaps to a fine bottle of wine with accompanying carafe. Not only will you have a gift when you need it, but if you give a crappy gift, you have more on hand to beef it up.

When choosing gifts, get stuff you want for yourself, so if you don't use them, it spells good news for you. Perhaps a book you wanted to read, a pricy ornament you admired but didn't want to buy for yourself, or a festive platter that compliments your dishware. Wrap them up, stick a Post-it on top saying what's inside, and keep it close by like you do any other emergency item, such as a fire extinguisher. I'd recommend under your tree for a quick grab for home invaders and a few in your trunk for those surprise attacks on the go.

During the gift-giving season, we all need a little holiday emergency kit so we're prepared for gift-giving malfunctions. And if luck is on our side, or we never open our doors to unexpected callers, we won't need all our supplies and we'll have a little giftie for ourselves. Lord knows after all the holidays have put us through, we certainly deserve it!

The Rules of Regifting

Regifting is a fairly new phenomenon of our time like superviruses and low-cal potato chips that cause rectal leakage. Generations back, when Christmas meant more than exchanging gifts with everyone you've ever crossed paths with, gifts were only exchanged with close family and friends. But now that the true meaning behind Christmas seems to be good will toward capitalism, gifts have become more of an obligation than a desire, and all meaning has been lost. Since gifts are given out as freely as genital warts during spring break, we're stuck with a handful of crappy presents we don't know what to do with. Hence the phenomenon of regifting was created.

To some, regifting is a perfect solution. It's seen as a wonderful way to recycle things people have no use for and make someone else happy. To others, however, regifting is a tacky tradition that's reserved for trailer trash and Britney Spears (sorry, is that redundant?).

Then there are those that fall between the extreme left and right side of the regifting fence. They're the independents of regifting and have some leeway in the matter. They feel it's perfectly acceptable to regift, as long as you're honest about it and inform the recipient that it was a gift you couldn't use. Or, you can also regift as part of that great New Year's party game called "White Elephant," where everyone brings a lousy wrapped gift, and you trade it for other people's crappy gifts (see resource section for the rules. It really is quite the fun time).

"I was a big regifter until I gave my friend Lisa a gift, and, as she was opening it, I remembered that she had given it to me last Christmas! She looked kind of stunned and point blank asked if she had given me this gift last year. I told her, yeah, but I liked it so much, I got one for her as well! She bought the lie, but I knew then and there that regifting was way too stressful."

—Elaine

If you are a believer in the regift giving game, there are some basic strategies to abide by so that the gift doesn't come back to bite you in the bee-hind.

Rule #1: As soon as the gift giver is gone, rewrap the present. And don't forget to remove the card. Nothing says "regift" faster than a Labor Day hostess gift with a Santa sticker gift tag.

Rule #2: Stick a note on it saying what's inside and who gave it to you so you'll never give it back to that person or accidentally bring it to a game of White Elephant if you know that person is coming.

Rule #3: Keep the gift in its original packaging. Any seasoned regifter will tell you it's a novice mistake to regift an item without the warranty or instructions.

Rule #4: If you're going to regift, be sure that the item is unused. Especially if it's something personal like bath towels (yuk!) or lingerie (double yuk!).

It's a Wrap!

Ahh, the olden days. A time when you'd call a company and actually speak to a human being. A time when kids could play outside without fear of being abducted. And a time when stores would not only sell gifts but actually wrap them for you! To paraphrase Dorothy when saying goodbye to the scarecrow, "I'm going to miss that one most of all." Especially around the holidays.

No longer can we buy a gift and watch the salesperson dress it to the nines with shiny paper and a frilly bow. These days, if we're very, very lucky, we're handed a flattened box, a wad of tissue paper, and a bow that's branded with the store's name. If only stores would realize we'd shop there all year round if they'd only supply wrapping service (and buy any article of clothing if it came with a size 6 label). True, we can still get our gift wrapped at a major department store, but it's not always easy. Usually their gift-wrapping department is located in the bowels of the building, next to the janitorial supply closet. You may think you've found a wrapping oasis, but be warned. These places come with long lines and high price tags. In fact, you could buy a whole roll of paper and a spool of ribbon for the price of having just one gift wrapped.

If you buy a gift online, it's common for them to provide a gift-wrapping service as well. Sure, you don't have to search the store to find the wrapping station or wait an eternity to have it wrapped, but it too can come with a heavy price tag. Most often it costs between $5 and $8 per box, and there may be limits on the number of items you can put in one box, so you're forced to pay for multiple boxes to be wrapped. To lessen the expense, Google the online store then type "gift wrapping code" or "gift wrapping coupon." During the holidays, you can sometimes find a code to have this service done for free.

If you don't want to pay the heavy markup fee for wrapping, you're left with no other option than to wrap the gifts yourself. If you don't consider yourself a good gift wrapper, there are some simple tips to follow to make any package look professionally done. Not only will this impress your friends, but it'll bump up the look of even the cheapest gift.

When it comes to buying wrapping paper, think simple. Stick with one color, like a festive red or sparkly silver. Then you can spruce it up with a wonderful bow, a message made out of alphabet stamps, or a sparkly design made with glue and glitter.

Clear or colored cellophane makes for an elegant look and easy wrapping. Just cut out a square large enough to gather around the gift and tie it up with a great bow.

Attach small objects to the ribbon such as a few jingle bells, a candy cane, a colorful ornament, or a small sprig of pine. You can even punch a hole in a card and string it through as well. Or print out a vintage photo from your computer and make that into a card.

Buy a roll of great ribbon. I like the kind with wire along the edges since it creates a professional-looking bow. Raffia is always a great choice and looks good on any package. Or, instead of ribbon, use colorful tape to tie around the package.

If, even with these suggestions, wrapping is just too frustrating, **stuff your present in a cute gift bag.** It's the "instant rice" of holiday wrapping.

One final note: If you're wrapping a gift for your kid from Santa, you should know that Santa is very anal about his wrapping style. Or at least some people think he is. When I wrapped our daughter's first presents from Santa, my husband had very specific instructions on how it needed to be done. The big gift had to be left unwrapped and put in front of the others. Then, the smaller gifts were to be wrapped, but they *must not* be wrapped in the same paper, ribbon, or tags as any other presents left under the tree. Keep in mind, our daughter wasn't old enough to find her thumb, yet my husband was adamant that the rules were followed to the letter. This is how he was brought up and gosh golly gonads, he was going to do the same thing for his offspring. So, if you have kids celebrating their first Christmas, check with your spouse before wrapping any gifts that may need to be redone. A mind, and wrapping paper, is a terrible thing to waste.

Chapter 6

deck the halls with tons of crap

Ahhh, Christmas decorations. What would the holidays be without the annual trip to the hardware store, discount depot, and home goods emporium to load up on more holiday crap to decorate our homes with? But how much is too much? Some of us just can't stop ourselves! We pack on so many layers of fluff, our house is transformed into something almost unrecognizable, like John Travolta in *Hair Spray*. Between the blinking lights, the singing lawn figurines, the shiny wreaths, and the blinding tree, your once conservative home now looks like a Vegas showgirl.

The stores understand our incessant need to buy more and more holiday decorations, which is why they start selling the stuff so early on in the year. And by early I mean during the Back to School sales. There's just something inherently wrong with loading up on both protractors and icicle lights at the same time.

I've always had a problem with stores selling things before we actually need them. I detest trying on wool sweaters on hot summer days. Or worse, stuffing my body into a skimpy bathing suit just when I've built up my winter layers of fat. With any luck, the stores will keep selling things earlier and earlier until finally, they catch up and sell things for the season we actually need them!

But until that time, get out your charge cards, head over to your mega mart, and load up your vehicles with even more gaudy decorations to make your home shine! Because, starting in the month of September, it's beginning to look a lot like Christmas!

A Quick History Lesson

The Christmas tree is no doubt the longest-standing holiday decoration in history. But like everything else that's centered around the holidays, it too has evolved. If you thought the first Christmas tree was purple aluminum and chock full of *I Love Lucy* collectable Hallmark ornaments, you're surely mistaken. So how did this tradition of sprucing up a spruce begin? Get out your number two pencils because I'm going to give you a history lesson about how the tradition of the Christmas tree came to be.

The ancient Romans were the first people known for decorating shrubbery, and they did it to impress Saturn, the god of agriculture. But it wasn't until the seventh century, however, that decorating a tree became associated with Christianity. That's when a monk came to pagan Germany to spread the word of Christ. For visuals, he needed something triangularly shaped to symbolize the Father, Son, and Holy Spirit. Since Cool Ranch Doritos hadn't been invented, he turned to the three-pointed structure of a tree.

"I bought a fresh tree and that night, my entire home was swarming with praying mantises. It seems they were lying dormant and the heat of my house made them come to life! I can't even look at a tree now without freaking out!"

—Katrina

In the sixteenth century, some Germans with an eye for interior design had the inspirational idea to bring the holiday tree indoors. Soon, all the "in" people were doing it, and adorning their trees with beautiful fruits, candles, and extravagant handmade ornaments, many of which can still be found for a hefty price on eBay.

When European descendants flocked to America, the Christmas tree was introduced. At that time, holiday trees were generally smaller, standing about four feet tall, but we Americans supersized our trees, preferring them to go from floor to ceiling. With the inventions of plastic and Wal-Mart, the beautiful, ornate ornaments were replaced by generic ones and mass-produced. And, since America is the melting pot of all races, we reflect that style by covering our trees in all the various colors of the rainbow.

That's it, students. The basic history of the Christmas tree. Now you know its evolution from being a gift to the gods, to being a gift to your pets by providing them with indoor plumbing. What the future holds, we can only imagine. But as long as they sell trees, and those vintage ornaments on eBay, I'm confidant the glorious tradition of the Christmas tree will continue.

A Tree Grows in Brooklyn ... and in Your Living Room

Although we Americans love our Christmas trees and insist on getting one every year, there are some challenges that come along with bringing a bit of the outdoors in. Especially if you don't have various family members to please. Here are some of the yearly battles you can count on having with your loved ones:

Which variety to choose: Pepsi vs. Coke. Mac vs. PC. Leno vs. Letterman. There always seems to be competition. In the tree world, the two heavy hitters are the noble against the fir. Everyone has their personal preference, and when there are multiple people to please, buying a tree can cause multiple problems. If you have heavy ornaments, I'd suggest going with a spruce, since it has stronger branches. It's also a good choice if your cat likes to use the tree as a scratching post because it has the sharpest needles. *Tip: no matter which variety you choose, run your hand through a branch to make sure the needles are soft and don't come off easily in your hand. Also, measure your room first so you know what size to get, and don't forget to add on the length of the tree-top ornament.

How much to spend: When it comes to the price of a tree, the sky's the limit. I know there's the cost of the seedling, the expense of watering it, cutting it down, and driving it to the big city, but the high price of trees is hard to understand. *Tip: If you want to save money, skip the private Christmas tree lots and head on down to your local home building store. Or buy one from a charitable organization. It may still cost a lot, but you're doing good to others.

Transporting it home. If you have an SUV with a luggage rack and two brawny he-men to help you load it onto the roof of your car, bringing your tree home will be easy. If not, the only way to bring home your ten-foot fir with your eight-foot compact is if you have a clown car feature. *Tip: when transporting your tree, decide which side will be facing the wall and put that side down on the top of your car.

Keeping the damn thing alive: Having a tree is like having a newborn! They both need constant attention. Okay, maybe not constant. But they both run the risk of dehydration. If you ever let the water bowl run dry, you're just a hop, skip, and jump away from sitting around a dead tree. *Tip: Be sure to cut off half an inch to the trunk when you buy it (the lot will often do this for you). This will give your tree at least two more weeks of freshness. Also, make sure to keep the bowl filled with water from the start since trees can absorb up to two gallons the very first day!

Putting up the lights: Everyone has their own particular style of hanging the lights and they're adamant that their way is the only right way to do it. Some string the lights up and down (my personal favorite). Others prefer to go in circles around the tree. And then there are those capable of decorating trees at Tavern on the Green who wrap each individual branch. *Tip: Store your lights on a roller to make them easy to wind and unwind every year (go to *www .treekeeperbag.com* to find one).

Disposing of the tree: Once the chore of taking the decorations off is done, what do you do with the tree carcass? If it's available in your area, recycle! *Tip: Some trees are sold in big plastic bags. If so, pull the bag down as soon as you set it up indoors and hide the bag underneath the tree skirt. Then, after Christmas, remove the skirt and pull the bag back up and transport it to a recycling center in your area. Not only is this good for the environment, it's good for your living room floor, since the bag will prevent the floor from being covered with pine needles.

No matter which variety you choose, how you decorate it, and where you dispose of it, the most important thing about a tree is that it doesn't cause your house to burn down. Be sure you use lights that are for indoor use, water it so it doesn't dry out, and set it up away from heaters and fireplaces! Don't use frayed wires, don't put chords underneath rugs, and don't use more than three sets of lights on one extension cord. I think we all can agree that a tree should bring you cheer, not char.

Faux Christmas

From snow in a can to aluminum trees, it's not just boobs that are fake anymore. We live in a phony world filled with imitation crab and laminate flooring. Leather is replaced with Pleather, rhinestones imitate real diamonds, and even hair is enhanced by extensions. This trend toward imitation has now seeped into the holidays as well.

In days past, you'd walk into a home decked out for the holidays, and be overwhelmed by the fresh scent of pine. Between the fresh garlands, the bright green wreathes, and the ten-foot noble, a home used to smell like a woodland forest. But now with the advent of plastic garlands and aluminum trees, that holiday smell is replaced by what can only be described as sticking your nose into an old Tupperware container. Instead of hanging a wreath covered in fresh moss, you hang a plastic pinecone motif by Target circa 1997. Instead of natural beeswax candles, the mantle is accented with plug-in faux candles from Restoration Hardware. Even the logs that burn in the fireplace are artificial and give off an unnatural blue flame.

Don't get me wrong. I understand why people have more plastic in their homes than Joan Rivers has on her face. Real don't come cheap. At my local Christmas lot, fresh garland sells for $1.35 a foot, and a small grouping of mistletoe costs five bucks! Who wants to dole out dough year after year when you can buy it once and have it outlast you? The downside, however, is that our children will never equate the smell of pine needles with the holidays. Instead, they'll associate it with the crunchy feel of aluminum between their fingers and the constant ring of the doorbell as a steady stream of UPS men make their deliveries.

Perhaps there's a happy medium. If you must use plastic decorations, enhance it with a bit of nature. Mix some fresh pine branches with the fake. If you can, use a variety called Grand Fir since it's known for being the most aromatic. If you're going to use battery-operated candles, light a few holiday-scented ones as well. If you mix some real along with the fake, you can have affordable decorations and a nice-smelling home. If it were only that easy to fix Joan Rivers's face.

House Lights

There's always one household in each neighborhood that keeps their Christmas lights up months after the holidays are over—sometime even year round. It's the house that all the neighbors

talk about. "Why does Jim keep those f*in' lights up all year?"
"Man, is he one s*it ass lazy mo-fo." (Guess Jim doesn't live in
the best neighborhood.) But the truth is that there are plenty of
advantages to keeping your lights up year round. Here are a few:

1. You travel a lot and it helps you find your house when
   you're flying over it at night.
2. Your wife always has to have something to nag you
   about, so this keeps her off your back about the trash
   or how you always fold the towels wrong.
3. You're not sure you believe in global warming so you figure
   you'll waste a lot of energy and see if anything happens.
4. You hate your neighbors and you know it drives them
   bananas.
5. You don't smoke pot anymore so you just take a big
   swig of cold medicine and watch the lights twinkle.
6. Okay, because you actually are a s*it ass lazy mo-fo.

Keeping Up with the Joneses Décor

During the hot summer months, homeowners have an unspo-
ken competition about whose lawn is the greenest. Neighbors come out in droves mowing, fertilizing, and watering
their lawn until they're as green as lime Jello. But in the
winter, when the ground is frozen, neighbors compete in a
different arena: whose yard had the most impressive display
of Christmas decorations.

Every year the gardening gloves come off and the work
gloves go on. Lights are hung, stakes are hammered, and
extension chords are plugged in. Ladders reach the highest branches and tallest rooftops. Like Christmas, holiday

displays get more and more opulent every year as manufacturers introduce new decorations. What were once a few
strands of colored lights hung on the front gutter now use
more wattage than Times Square. And the once lowly plastic
Santa has evolved into a yard full or robotic characters, special effects, and music blasting from hidden speakers. The
only thing missing is Splash Mountain.

The madness of decoration doesn't stop with the neighbors.
Now entire neighborhoods get in on the deal. Every metropolis
has its own version of "Candy Cane Lane," where city blocks get
in on the insanity. Visitors come out in droves to see them, and
the gridlock traffic becomes a nightmare. If you want to see a
Candy Cane Lane in your area, just look up in the sky at night,
since the lights from the displays and headlights shine with
such intensity, it looks like a friggin' Batman signal!

Like everything from body piercings to teenage promis-
cuousness, it's time for the pendulum to start swinging the
other way. Sure it's nice to decorate your home for Christmas,
but in an age of high energy costs and depleting resources,
think quality, not quantity. Plus, there is something to the
adage "less is more." It might not ring true for the serving
size of pecan pie, but when it comes to the amount of holiday decorations, I think there's something to it.

"We would always go all out on decorations because my kid wanted
our house to be the best decorated one on the block. But then we
got new neighbors who had their house professionally done and it
was like living next door to the Macy's parade. We finally gave up."

—Steve

I'm Dreaming of a Green Christmas

Global warming alert: Between the millions of trees being cut down for wrapping paper and the excess wattage wasted on lights, the North Pole will be melted by New Year's!

I can't talk about the holidays without talking about holiday waste. The Environmental Protection Agency estimates that between Thanksgiving and New Year's Day, household waste goes up 25 percent. Americans produce an extra 200,000,000 pounds of extra garbage . . . *each week*! It's one thing to waste time and money during the holidays, but wasting the environment is another.

One of the biggest assaults is the use, or should I say misuse, of paper. Between wrapping paper and shopping bags, we waist a total of 4 million *tons*! One thing we can do to reduce the amount is buy cards and gift wrapping made from recycled paper, and recycle paper ourselves. Also, wrap gifts creatively using saved paper from other gifts, or consider nonpaper wrapping like large leaves, cloth, or even used dryer sheets. Skip the gift tag and write the name of the recipient directly on the wrapped present. And instead of all that ribbon, just stick on a small festive bow. If every person saved two feet of ribbon during the holidays, it'd be enough to wrap around the planet!

Many people try to be green by skipping that live tree and going with an artificial one. They feel by doing this, they'll do their part to save the rain forest. But the fact is that most all trees sold during the holidays are grown on a Christmas tree farm and are periodically replaced, so they're not a detriment to the environment. Plus, if they're recycled, they become mulch, which saves water in your garden. Not only are real trees good, but artificial ones are actually harmful since they're made of polyvinyl chloride (PVC) which creates pollution. Some of them, especially older imitation trees, have been known to contain lead. Some tree huggers go one step further and buy living trees and bring them inside to decorate. The problem is that live trees can only stay indoors between four to ten days without being harmed, and then they should go back outside. Plus, the whole environmental advantage of live trees is that they can be planted outdoors after the holidays, but since they can grow up to sixty feet, you'd need to live on a golf course to have the extra yard space!

One of the best ways to be environmentally sound is to purchase LED-type lights to decorate your tree and home exterior. These lights were introduced in 2001 and are 90 percent more effective than the old fashioned kind. On average, it costs $10 to light a Christmas tree using older bulbs, but if you swapped them out for LED lights, it would only cost fifteen cents. That's a huge savings, people! According to one U.S. Department of Energy study, if everyone replaced their old lights with LED ones, it would save at least 2 billion kilowatt-hours of electricity for the month of December (and even more if you include lazy people who don't take down their lights until St. Patrick's Day). That's enough to supply energy to 200,000 homes for an entire year! Plus, LED lights aren't hot to the touch so they reduce fire risks and painful owies to curious little fingers.

In the spirit of giving this season, why not give a gift to Mother Earth and think green. In return, she'll thank you with a cleaner planet, fresher air, and a polar ice cap that won't fall in the ocean causing mass destruction and the end of mankind as we know it. Mother Nature gives nice thank-you gifts!

Where to Store All the Crap

When looking for a new home, most people want enough bedrooms and bathrooms to accommodate the size of their family, plus enough kitchen counter space to display their kitschy rooster collection. But what's often overlooked is the huge amount of storage space needed to house holiday decorations. Unless you live in the Spelling mansion, chances are you're not going to have the room for all this crap.

Every year when you collect yet another piece of holiday memorabilia, you don't think ahead as to where it will be stored post-Christmas. And why should you? When you buy large items such as lawn decorations, they come neatly folded in a manageable-sized cardboard box. But once you take it out of its original packaging, it expands like a blowup raft. You can never get everything back inside the box unless you have the folding powers of a salesperson at The Gap.

Not only do you have the large lawn decorations to contend with, you also have the lights, the Christmas tree stand (and tree if you use an artificial one), your growing ornament collection, the decorated tree skirt, the reindeer dishware, your faux wreaths and garlands, the stockings you hung by the chimney with care, plus all the stuff you bought during the after Christmas sale for the following year when everything was 50 percent off. On second thought, maybe the Spelling mansion isn't big enough!

So the question remains, where the heck do you put all this stuff? The few storage closets you have are already busting at the seams with Halloween decorations and old boxes filled with stuff you can't bring yourself to toss, like your old retainer and your first driver's license. And even if you do have the room, how do you store all the junk so it won't get ruined?

To help you on *where* to put your stuff, go to an organizer store and check out their unique containers to house holiday crap. They sell specialty boxes and bags for artificial trees, ornaments, wreathes, and lights. These stores may be pricy, so here are some ways to do the same thing for less:

- **An artificial tree:** Stick it in a double strength trash bag and call it a day.
- **Ornaments:** Use a cardboard box used to house a case of wine. Just use padding between each ornament to prevent it from scratching or breaking. You can also use an egg carton or plastic cups with shredded paper.
- **Your wreath:** Hang it on a hanger, cover it with a plastic bag, and hang it in the back of your closet.
- **Holiday candles:** Wrap in bubble wrap, or, just stick them in an old sock.
- **Lights:** Cut slits in the top and bottom of an empty wrapping paper tube. Stick the socket in the top slit and wrap around and around, sticking the end in the bottom slit.

Chapter 7

i'll be home for christmas ... if i can get through the f*cking crowds

In generations past, all we did to get to grandmother's house was go over the river and through the woods. But now, traveling to our relatives during Christmas entails jet engines, four wheel drives, and bumper-to-bumper traffic. Every winter there are blizzards and ice storms and hail that cause long airport delays and five-car pileups making it impossible to get around. Yes sir-eee, traveling and winter do not mix, and when you try to force them together, you get missed connections, slick road conditions, and the complete opposite of a very merry Christmas.

So why do we do it? Why do we take that pilgrimage back to our extended family year after year, and suffer through the slings and arrows of outrageous torture? For some, it's because their love of family far outweighs any travel hassles. For others it's because of the all-consuming guilt they'll experience if they don't go. Yup. One hundred percent gut-wrenching, mama-induced, stronger than that brand of tequila with the worm inside guilt! As bad as holiday traveling can be, it ain't nothing compared with having to endure the silent treatment, the heavy sighs, or worse, the "I understand, dear" when you know deep down she's thinking "I spent sixteen hours in hard labor and have the hemorrhoids to prove it and you can't even deal with a crowded airport?"

I have a thought. Since there's no proof that Christ was actually born on December 25, why go through all the hassle at all? You don't believe me? Go ahead and check the Bible. I defy you to find his exact date of birth. In fact, there's controversy that Jesus was even born in December at all. Saint Luke said that shepherds watched over their flocks by night when he was born, and shepherds only watched flocks by night when there were lambs. Since lambs are only around in the spring, I see that as enough evidence to cancel your trip and rebook it for the spring when the weather is nice and shiny. Shy of that, here are some ways to make any trip during the holidays smoother sailing.

Hub Sweet Hub

Oh man. You didn't listen to me and planned a trip during the busy holiday season. And by air, no less, where you have absolutely no control over the weather, the departure times, or the on-board movie. What are ya, nuts? If you simply must fly during the holidays, there are some things you should know to make your travels less tumultuous.

Top Ten Rules to Almost Survive Air Travel

1. Book your ticket early (although if you're looking for a way out of your family get-togethers, wait until the last minute, when there are no seats available)!

2. Take alternate airports. Sure some of the smaller ones may be farther away, but they're goldmines. They have smaller terminals that are easy to maneuver, and more affordable nearby parking. Some even offer on-lot, valet parking where you get your car cleaned and return to one less errand upon your return. Not only is parking easier, but you may also save on car rental and nearby hotels. It's like living in Mayberry!

3. To prevent lost luggage, consider shipping your bags ahead. If you *do* check them, be sure to tag it with your name and phone numbers (don't use your address since you'll risk being robbed while you're away). Also, know the rules about carry-on baggage regarding size and weight. The last thing you want is have to check your bag with your medications and trashy novel.

4. At all costs, avoid layovers and fly direct. If you have to make a connection, be sure to allow at least an hour between flights to avoid missed connections and therefore, lost luggage.

5. Book your seat assignment when you book your ticket to assure that you're not away from your spouse or children . . . or, perhaps not!

6. If your plane is delayed because of anything other than weather, try invoking rule 240. This states that the airlines must book you on the next available plane to your destination, whether it be on another airline or

even in first class. This rule mostly pertains to older airlines, but it's always worth a try.

7. Don't bring wrapped gifts! The last thing you want is for it to be unwrapped at security and have little Johnny discover that you got him a hot wheels track right before boarding a plane. Not only will he beg you for the duration of the flight to set it up, but if it's what he wanted from Santa, you're screwed.

8. Give yourself plenty of time for check in. That's always the hard part for me. I don't want to get there too early that I go stir crazy, yet so late that I lose five years of my life span due to stress.

9. Be sure to bring some antibacterial wipes for the armrests and eating tray in hopes of killing any nasty germs. Traveling is one thing. Traveling when you're sick is a whole different ball of wax.

10. And the number one way to survive air travel during the holidays…DON'T DO IT! Feign sickness, stay home, and save yourself!

Upgrade Your Trip

If you're going to fly, you'll enjoy your experience a hell of a lot more if you're in first class rather than economy. There, you're allowed to board early, get a drink before take off, have scrumptious food not available to the mere peons, have a reclining seat that actually reclines, and be constantly asked if you want your drink refilled! Ahhh, now that's livin'! In first class you don't even worry that the plane will go down because you'll already be in heaven!

Unfortunately, not everyone can afford to fly in first class (or even business class) but, if you play your cards right, your tush may find itself nestled in one of these coveted leather-clad cushions. How? It's called an "upgrade," and it's the Golden Ticket of airline travel awarded only to those lucky few who are savvy enough to play the system. To let you in on some of the tricks in the flying trade, here are some ways to get the prize of an upgrade:

When you buy your ticket, don't get the cheapest one. You'll notice your ticket has an alphabetic code telling the airlines how much you spent. If you have one that's ranked Y or higher, you'll have a better chance of getting an upgrade than if you got a nonrefundable budget fare.

Dress for success. As they say, clothes make the man, and you hope they make the man behind the ticket counter think you're worthy of an upgrade when you ask for one.

Be sure to join the airline's mileage program. It's free and you'll have a greater chance of getting an upgrade if you're a member of the club (if you earn enough miles on your card, you always have the option of using any accrued miles to upgrade).

Arrive at the airport early and request an upgrade when you first check in. Hopefully, first come, first upgraded.

Leave your kids with another member of your party. Although your kids may be the apple of your eye, they could be the thorn in someone's side in the air. Just say, "My companions and I would like to see if we can be upgraded."

If you're making a connecting flight and you had some problems with the first flight, politely tell that to the agent. He or she might upgrade you if you have a legitimate complaint.

And finally, board late. If there are any upgrades available, the agents may scan the area for any last-minute upgrades.

Traveling with Kids Sucks

This horrific aspect of the holidays can be a book on its own. Any parent who has flown the friendly skies knows just how unfriendly they can be when you bring your baby on board. Depending on the age of your offspring, you can expect everything from misery, embarrassment, frustration, and a cabin full of unwanted bodily fluids. Even the powers of those fish-shaped crackers aren't strong enough to save you.

Flying with kids is never a good thing. The pressure of the ascent causes their tiny ears to become painful. Minutes later, boredom sets in and quickly leads to crying and frustration (for both you and your kid). For a child, an airline flight is a constant "no" fest at 3,200 feet. "No, you can't unbuckle your seatbelt!" "No, you can't run around the airplane!" "No, you can't ask out the flight attendant" (. . . oh wait, that one's for your husband). A novice parent would try to appease their kid with sugar, but any seasoned flyer knows that once a sugar rush sets in, you're setting up a scarier situation than *Snakes on a Plane*.

If you're on the return trip, things get even worse. Kids are usually exhausted from their trip, especially if you've crossed over a time zone. And, as any parent knows, when your kid doesn't sleep well, everyone is tired and cranky. Combine these factors and stick your kids in cramped quarters for hours on end, and you've got the fixings for a true aviation disaster.

To avoid this catastrophe, here are some suggestions:

If given a choice, book tickets on an airline that has TV reception and a personal monitor. Some good ones are Jet Blue, Frontier, Virgin America, and Virgin Atlantic. I'm also quite fond of Midwest Airlines, which, for a minimal fee, offers a personal handheld monitor that's loaded with movies for both kids and grownups, plus some TV shows.

Since kids can be finicky eaters, and airlines rarely offer food anymore, bring healthy snacks. Ideally the snacks should take some time to eat, like dry cereal from a cup eaten one at a time. If you're going to offer sugar treats, think lollipops instead of cookies, since they take a long time to consume.

Bring plenty of age-appropriate toys to occupy them, some favorites from home plus a few surprises. Avoid toys that play music, since they'll drive you or other passengers crazy, or ones with little parts, since they tend to fall on the floor and are hard to pick up. If your kids are too young to play with toys, chew bubblegum and blow bubbles. Babies love bubbles. It's their version of a Steve Carell movie.

Make sure you board the plane with your kid in a clean diaper. It's hard to change a diaper in a small airplane bathroom. Sometimes international flights have changing tables, but I wouldn't count on one for a domestic flight. Then you have the whole "where should I put this dirty diaper anyway?" For that, bring some quart-size freezer bags with you to store the dirty diapers and lock in the stink. Then, ask the steward where to dispose of it. In most cases, it'll be in the galley trash.

If your kids are old enough, try booking the bulkhead seat. There's extra room for your kids to sit and play. Don't get seats on an exit row since only children over the age of fifteen are allowed to sit there.

If you're bringing a car seat, make sure it's FAA approved if you're going to put your kid in there on the plane. For these and other safety tips, log onto *www.airsafe. com.* If you're only bringing the car seat because you're renting a car when you arrive, call the rental car company. Many offer car seats that you can rent.

Some airlines, like Virgin America, offer personal outlets for electrical appliances such as DVD players and bottle warmers.

Bring your stroller, bring your stroller, bring your stroller, bring your stroller! It's nice to have one with a storage bin underneath to free your hands of any carry-ons as you schlep through the airport. Almost all airlines will allow your stroller as a courtesy item. You keep your lil' one in it all the way up the ramp, then it's taken away, only to be waiting for you as you exit the plane! I tell ya, it's the best thing to hit airline travel since cocktail service.
If your child has complained of ear pain in the past after a flight, try a product called Ear Planes. They're like earplugs that are worn on ascent and descent.

Bodily fluids happen, so keep a change of clothes handy for both you and your baby.

If you child has a cold before your trip, visit his pediatrician to be sure he doesn't have an ear infection. If he does, the trip's off, since flying with an ear infection can cause the infection to get worse. If you're visiting your in-laws, just use this excuse anyway. What? They'll never know. You didn't actually tell your husband you could have sex after your six-week check up, did you?

Car Trouble

If you think traveling by air sucks during the holidays, traveling by car isn't a day at the beach either, unless you mean one of those days where you get stung by a jelly fish, slice your foot open on a buried beer can, and get sand embedded in crevices that only a gynecologist can see. The only way to make car travel bearable is if you drive on Christmas Day itself, when the roads are as wide open as . . . well, as your legs are during that gyno visit.

The holidays give people more reasons to drive. There are parties to go to. Shopping to do. And liquor stores to frequent when staying with relatives. It's no wonder the streets are packed. And, if you live in an area that's covered with ice and snow, the traffic's even worse. Everywhere you turn, there are dangerous road conditions and accidents to gawk at due to these dangerous road conditions. It's a wonder we can maneuver around the streets at all.

"I live in New Zealand, where it's summer in December. I wish I had the great excuse of bad weather to get me out of seeing my family during Christmas, but somehow, risking heavy perspiration just doesn't quite cut it."

—Gus

With that said, there are some guidelines to follow to make your trip easier. First, before you leave your garage, know the route you're going to travel. Check your local traffic Web sites to see if there's been an accident or blockade to avoid. If you have one of those newfangled GPS devices that offer up-to-the-minute traffic conditions, it's a great way to avoid current roadblocks. Also, be sure to leave early, especially on getaway weekends or coming-home days. Keep your car well maintained with plenty of fluids and good tires that are properly inflated. If you're a member of an auto club, don't forget to bring your card. And be sure that your cell phone is charged and that you have a car charger if you're going on a long trip.

If you have kids in the back, have an old fashioned sing-along to keep them entertained! Yeah, right. If you suggested that, I think they could legally shoot you. These days car travel with kids is all about a portable DVD player, a video iPod, and a Nintendo DS with multiple games. Sure, there's absolutely no family bonding, but at least they'll keep their traps shut so you won't have to endure hours of "Mom, she's touching me!" or the classic, "Are we there yet?"

If your kids get carsick, roll down the window, have them sit in the center and look forward. If they're old enough, have them sit up in front. If nothing else works, try Drama-mine. We call it Drama-queen in our house because it makes our daughter tired and emotional, turning her into an evil she-devil. But at least she's not puking all over the car. They sell less drowsy formulas but don't expect miracles.

Yes, driving during the holiday season can be a struggle. But if you're prepared, know where you're going, and have a well-maintained vehicle and kids that aren't barfing in the back seat, it can make any road you travel a whole lot smoother.

Once Is Always Enough

As if traveling in late December isn't bad enough, many people have to do it several times during one holiday season. If you come from a family with divorced parents, chances are you have to double dip and split your time. You have to visit your your dad, his new bride, and their new baby, whom he constantly dotes on, when all the attention you got as a kid was the occasional "I've got your nose" trick. Afterward, you must hit the road again and visit mom and her shack-up boyfriend that she doesn't want to commit to because she's afraid to walk down the aisle after going through all that pain, thank you very much.

Then there's the scenario where your parents are divorced, you're divorced from your first husband with whom you had kids, and now you're remarried to someone else and have added more babies to your collection. If you have a lot of baggage, or you're married to someone that does, rest assured you'll be packing a lot of baggage come the holidays.

And while we're on the subject of multiple travel, what about the situation where you have to take multiple modes of transportation to get to one destination? For instance, I married a man from Humansville, Missouri. During the holidays, we fight bumper-to-bumper traffic to go to LAX (1 hour), check in luggage, go through security, and wait for our plane (1 hour), then travel to Denver since, surprise, surprise, there is no direct flight to Humansville (2 hours), wait the layover (2 hours), fly to Kansas City (1:40 minutes), take the shuttle bus to the rental car dealership and get a car (1 hour), then drive to my in-law's place (3 hours)! That's eleven hours and forty minutes, people! And that's if our layover is *ONLY* two hours because oftentimes, with the weather delays or missed connections, it can be a whole lot longer (note to self: husband number two must have parents that live close to an airport hub).

We both know I've been using a lot of lists this chapter on how to deal with problems, and I'm not going to put you through that again. Besides, I don't really have any solution on how to avoid multiple travel destinations by keeping families together. There've been plenty of marriage counselors and Dr. Laura shows before me that have tried. My best advice is to be safe, plan ahead, and if you're dating a man from a small town, check out the holiday commute to visit the in-laws before you commit.

Check Out Ways to Check In Easier

Okay, you got me. I'm not a worldly traveler. In the past ten years, the only place our family has gone is to Humansville. And, since my husband says his relatives would be hurt if we were to stay anyplace other than their home, I'm not a hotel expert either. But, for the sake of research, we took a family vacation this Christmas to New York City. Not only did this allow me the opportunity to do research for this book, but I also got to travel to someplace other than Humansville and for that, I'm incredibly grateful.

Since hotels are not my forte, I turned to Steven Pipes, managing director for the famous Le Parker Meridien Hotel in New York. It's a gorgeous hotel smack dab in the middle of all the action. But besides being gorgeous, it has the added dimension of being one of the most kid-friendly hotels in Manhattan. Steven told me some inside information about how to book hotels, what kind of hotels to book, and how to get the best rate, all of which I'll share with you now.

Steven's tips:

If you're traveling with kids and not sure which hotel to book, go to Google and type in the city you're traveling to and then "kid-friendly hotels." Go to the Web sites that come up and check out what they offer for kids. Le Parker Meridien for example, offers in-room games, a pool, coloring books, cartoons in the elevators, razor scooter rentals, and restaurants with a kids' menu including yummy options you'd want for yourself but would be too embarrassed to order except when you're with your kids.

Don't rely too heavily on online reviews. It's not unusual for hotels to give themselves high praise, or competitors to give them low ones.

Although you usually pay more for a great location, it may actually save you money in the long run if you're staying in a big city. That's because you won't pay more for taxis or car rentals to get to the places you want to be.

Although there are many reputable Internet sites for booking hotels, you can get the same price by calling the hotel directly and not the 800 number. The only exception is when the Web site says "Internet-only deals" which are usually more restrictive.

If the hotel you want to stay at says they're full, keep checking their Web site for openings since cancellations are common.

If the hotel has a concierge service, use it! I had no idea what these people are there for, and it seems they're there for me (I guess my parents were right when they told me I'm special)! Not only are they helpful for basic things like directions, but they can also get you tickets to local events, book dinner reservations, give you insider tips on the city, and may even provide coupons to popular tourist attractions.

If you're going out of town during the holidays and need to book a hotel, take Stephen's advice. And if you have kids, be sure to stay at a place that not only welcomes them, but also keeps them entertained. And a good kids' menu doesn't hurt either. Everyone enjoys a good chocolate chip waffle from time to time!

"We booked our hotel room online and the room looked great. When we got there, it was the same room and all, but it didn't look nearly as good. I never realized when hotels took photos of their rooms, that they lit them like they were models."

—Glen

family squabbles: all we want is a silent night

Show of hands please ... how many of you grew up with two loving parents and caring siblings who protected you from bullies on the playground? Not many, huh. Now let me see how many were raised by loony birds who had no business taking care of houseplants, let alone kids, and had brothers and sisters whose only use for you was to blame things on you when they did something wrong? Yup. Just what I thought.

That's why it's no mystery that getting together with the people you grew up with can bring up all the suppressed feelings of your childhood. As soon as you cross over that family threshold during the holidays, you instantly regress back into a child. If you think that makes for a fun family event, think again. Instead, it makes for resentment, squabbles, and the reason why people spike eggnog when it's a rather delicious beverage all on its own.

If you feel like you're the only person who detests getting together with their loved ones, take comfort in the fact that you're not alone. It's actually a very common conundrum. And although I can't provide instant fixes for problems that took decades to evolve, I can provide a few helpful hints, and a couple of jokes, in hopes of making the holiday get-togethers easier to bear.

The Explosion of the Nuclear Family

Since half of all marriages end in divorce, half of all holidays end in disaster. When that nuclear family is torn apart, gone are the family traditions and lovely Norman Rockwell moments. No longer are Mom, Dad, little Danny, and baby Jane opening presents around the glowing tree while Christmas carols play in the background. Instead, Dad gets the kids on his court-appointed day while Mom nurses her third gin and tonic wondering how her bastard of an ex spent their entire nest egg on dirtypanties.com without her ever knowing.

Anyone who's gone through a divorce knows just how bad it can suck. And it's never more apparent than during the holidays—or birthdays, or Sunday night dinners, or hell, on plain stinkin' Tuesdays. Not only does divorce affect the nuclear family, but also like all nuclear explosions, it destroys everything in its path. The mothers- and fathers-in-law are bitter because they have less time with their grandkids. The aunts and uncles are pissed off because they don't have their nieces and nephews around on family visits, so they're forced to play with their own damn kids. And there's resentment toward the spouse that left, making everyone take sides. Yup. It sucks all right.

As you can imagine, all this tension and suckiness makes sitting in a room together during the holidays quite strained. And because no one wants to create a scene, especially when the kids are around, feelings are bottled up. Conflict is avoided, and the pressure builds. But as anyone who's ever tried to hold in a fart knows, you can only hold things inside for so long. You try with all your might, but then it comes out at the dinner table causing a terrible stink—and I'm not talking about the fart. Pleasant chit-chat is replaced with emotional tirades, and memories are created that you'd rather forget.

He Gets Holidays

When it's *not* your turn with the kids, a white Christmas turns as black as your mood. It's guaranteed depression that cuts so deep you thank God there are hotlines and Milano cookies around to get you through these difficult times. You can't go to restaurants or malls because the sight of happy children frolicking with their parents is too much to bear. You can't even watch TV because of the dang Christmas specials that you used to watch with your kids every year. You stare at your flickering tree that you put up for your kids when they come over, and hope it's bigger and brighter than the one "he" has.

So how do you make it through another Christmas? While there's nothing that can take the pain away completely that doesn't require a prescription pad or a giant swig of Nyquil that surpasses the recommended dosage, there are some things that might numb it for a while.

Surround yourself with other divorced parents. They know just what you're going through and can offer a lot of support. And when they don't have their kids either, you can hang out together, which sure beats hanging out alone. You can laugh and cry and make voodoo dolls of your exes and put them in the freezer to stop them from moving on in life. It's great fun!

Stay busy. Easier said than done, I know. But force yourself to get out of the house.

Volunteer. Lord knows there are charities around that need help. Not only will this keep you busy (see tip #2) but seeing those who endure such hardships can put your life in perspective.

Don't feel guilty about the kids. Yes, it can be hard for them, but guilt will do them no good. Hey, they get two Christmases, and for a kid, that's the trifecta of holidays. Resist the urge to compete with your ex. Instead of trying to get the most expensive gift, do things with your kids on Christmas like a puzzle or craft if they're young, or make a movie from your freshly shot Christmas video on your computer. These really are the things they'll remember.

Do your kids a favor and don't fight with you ex in front of them, don't make them pick sides, and don't have them miss an important event just because it's your turn to be with them and you're going to make them, gosh dang darn it. Instead, talk with your ex about what you both can do to make their holidays as pleasant as possible. Let your kids call the parent they're not with on Christmas morning if they want. And if you can muster the strength, get your ex a gift and make sure the kids see you give it to him.

Granted, I know even with these tips, your holidays will be just a wee bit better than de-veining a big bag of raw shrimp, but perhaps it will take just a little of the sting away. Only time, and a lot of Milanos, will make any real difference.

Holiday Hilton

I admit it. I hate houseguests. I don't care if they're my friends and family, or my husband's. I'm just not one for having people stay in my home for any length of time. We don't have a guest room, so our kid has to sleep in our bed. We don't have an extra car, so I have to cart visitors all over the city. And we don't have an extra television set, so I have to watch *their* programs and miss my regular shows. I've heard it said that houseguests are like fish and go bad after four days, but I equate them more to mayonnaise on a hot summer's day. One hour max and things go rotten.

During the holidays, it's hard enough dealing with the stresses of the outside world let alone having to bring the stresses indoors by turning your home into a Hilton. I understand why houseguests happen. Staying in hotels is expensive, and the holidays are pricy enough without having to include a minibar tab. But sometimes guests stay with you simply because they just don't believe in staying in hotels. Perhaps they think they're nasty with unwashed sheets and mold-infested towels (although they've gotta be cleaner than my stuff). Or perhaps they think they'll offend me if they stay in a hotel (guess what? They won't!)

When guests are around, they always need to be entertained, and they always need to be fed. They wake up too early or go to bed too late because of the time difference. Plus, they don't know the idiosyncrasies of your home, so

they stuff the garbage disposal full of dried-up lasagna noo-
dles, not knowing that it's as sensitive as an ulcer patient and
can only handle soft food. Then it's busted, and you can't get
a repair guy out during the holidays, no way, no how!

That being said, if you must have people stay with you, here
are some ideas to make it better . . . not good, mind you, just
better:

**When you invite guests to stay (assuming you actually
invite them and not the other way around), tell them
how long they can stay.** I know it'll be tough, but say
something like, "Why don't you come on the twenty-first
and stay until the twenty-sixth?" Or, "Sorry, but you can't
come before the nineteenth because we have to deal with
some mold problems."

**If you don't have enough beds, invest in a blowup mat-
tress.** They've come a long way since they were only used
on camping trips, and now some versions even come with a
mock box spring.

**If the reason your guests don't spring for a rental car is
because they say they don't know their way around the
city, have them rent one with a GPS system.** If they say
that a car rental is too expensive, tell them that it's cheaper
if they don't get it at the airport (which is true) and you'll be
happy to take them to the dealership in town.

**Before they arrive, write down a list of the quirks in your
home,** like a slow shower drain, so you won't find yourself
stepping in a puddle of water on your hardwood floors outside
the bathroom.

"When my husband's family stayed with us, they were scattered all over the house and our young daughter had to sleep in our room. My husband was adamant that we all stay in our room until we heard his family wake up. Our four-year-old would throw tantrums because she was hungry, but he still didn't budge. After they left, my husband and I had to see a marriage counselor to discuss his priorities."

—Stephanie

Mom and Pop Quiz

Since no one really knows what goes on behind closed doors, how do you really know if your family is more whacked-out than other families? Who knows? Maybe everyone wishes they can take a chain saw to their family tree and cut off a few rotten branches. If you're not sure how your family ranks in the crazy hierarchy, here's a simple test to determine if your family is full of fun, or full of dysfunction:

1. Last Christmas, your uncle got your thirteen-year-old daughter:
a. a Hannah Montana CD
b. a pair of thong underwear
c. some class C narcotics

2. Last Christmas your Aunt Rhoda begged you to:
a. take a hundred bucks to buy yourself something nice
b. feel her new implants

c. let her stay with you for just a few months until her boss forgets about the embezzlement mishap

3. Your seventeen-year-old-niece just announced:
a. she got into an Ivy League school!
b. she's dropping out to pursue her dream of being manager at Limited 2
c. she's in love with some dude she met on a clubpenguin.com chat room and is pregnant with, what she's pretty sure is, his baby

If you answered mostly "a," your family isn't as bad as you thought, and you stand a darn good chance of having a happy holiday together. If you answered mostly "b," your family is a bit twisted and I'd advise you to always carry a flask wherever you go. If "c" was your answer of choice, your family is totally dysfunctional and I recommend you spend the holidays with the Kardashians. Sure, they're dysfunctional too, but at least you'd get some rockin' and expensive gifts!

Reconcilable Differences

If you're a couple, arguing during the holidays is very commonplace. If you don't believe me, just come over to my house in the month of December and I'll prove it to you. There, you'll find my husband and I arguing over our annual holiday hot topics such as the "you got to use tinsel last year, so this year I don't want to" feud or the "can you string the lights outside already so we have time to enjoy them?" debate. But by far, our loudest yuletide struggle has got to be about the presents.

I don't know why it is that when you walk down the aisle and promise to "love, honor, and cherish" the person, you somehow promise to take on dozens of other things as well. You promise to clean those nasty hairs out of the bathroom sink each day, and keep track of where the hell his damn wallet is. But during the holidays, you also promise to let him sit on his ass all month and watch football while you do all the cooking and cleaning. You promise to pick up all his visiting relatives while he's busy doing other important things . . . like the sitting on his ass thing. And the worst Christmas promise of all, you promise to buy all the freakin' gifts for his side of the family 'til death do you part! My husband is one of six kids who are all married with kids of their own, some of which also have kids of their own. It's like having to buy presents for the entire city of Scranton.

Because of frustrations you have with your significant other, there are significant problems during the holidays. Not only because there's so much to do and so much money to spend, but also because you're together a lot more, with school break and work vacation. It's cold outside, so you stay indoors more, which means someone is inevitably sick. Plus, Christmas is a time of great visitors, and whenever you mix marriage and family staying in your home, nothing good ever comes from it.

"When I was single, it always sounded so romantic to be with someone during the holidays. But now that I'm married all my husband and I ever seem to do is fight. It's like you have to choose between being lonely or pissed off."

—Robin

If you and your mate haven't mated in a while because of your bitterness and feuding around the holidays, take a breath and realize that there's probably nothing wrong with your relationship. It's just that it's being pushed to the limit. Time will pass, relatives will disperse, and lights will be put away (although never in the time frame you want them to be). A new year will begin and with it, will come a breath of fresh air to give CPR to your dying relationship.

Learn from your past. Before you sweep up the last of the dead pine needles, take out a piece of paper and devise a plan for next year. Both of you can write down your biggest frustrations and propose ways of dealing with them. Suggest sharing the workload so one of you isn't overwhelmed while the other one's biggest frustration is bedsores on their ass area. If it's financial frustrations, suggest ways to limit spending and stick to a budget (see page 26 for ideas). If it's relatives that are wearing you thin, agree in advance on how long they can visit. Once that list is done, pack it away with your Christmas decorations so that next year you can open that box before the holiday stress begins and keep your promise to love each other 'til death do you part!

Porn for Housewives

Christmas is a universal offender and is stressful to all people, but it seems to be the most stressful for married women with children. Many studies show that, whether or not both parents work, women still do the brunt of the household duties and child rearing obligations. And when the extra burden of the holidays comes along, wives carry around so much extra weight that they crumble.

Come Christmastime, women around the world stop fantasizing about romantic interludes with George Clooney, Russell Crowe, or Matthew Broderick (is it just me, or is that guy really hot?), and start fantasizing about something much more exciting: Their husbands taking on all the obligations of Christmas! They envision them doing all the shopping and errands and cooking and cleaning, and they work themselves into a tizzy of delight. Here are some of my own personal fantasies that really get me going:

My husband finally going to our kid's preschool Christmas party carrying a bag of his own homemade cookies. Of course, he'll inadvertently put peanuts in the cookies since he's never read any of the thousands of school notices warning about the perils of peanut allergies, and cause several children to go into anaphylactic shock.

My husband scouring the mall to buy gifts for my side of the family, then, asking me again and again to please sign my name on the accompanying Christmas cards that he struggled to write so that he could go to the post office and send the presents so they'd arrive in time. Of course, I'd tell him that I'd get to them eventually, stop bugging me, and then finally do it at the last second when the lines at the post office are the longest and the price to mail them is the highest.

My husband taking the kids to see Santa, including our potty-training toddler, who, after waiting an eternity in line to see Santa, has to go potty, *now*. Since Daddy rarely deals with potty-training emergencies, he'll erroneously think our kid can just "hold it," finding out that he can't when our kid takes a piss all over Santa.

My husband sitting in rush hour, bumper-to-bumper traffic with my visiting parents, hearing all the boring stories about distant relatives he's never met, as he schleps them to the most crowded tourist attractions in the city, during the busiest holiday weekend, with no parking, and long lines. Oh goodie. More time for stories.

My husband going to the supermarket on Christmas Eve to buy the sweet potatoes for the traditional Christmas Eve dinner casserole he's going to make, after forgetting the potatoes the first time he went to the supermarket that morning. He waits in the long line in the express lane deciding whether or not to make an issue of the dozen or so people ahead of him who have more than twelve items in their cart, but are trying to slide them through under the radar.

I can't go on any longer. I'm so turned on I feel like a teenaged boy at the Grotto pool at the Playboy Mansion! Oh, how I wish my fantasies will come true, but, like the one my husband has of me wearing nothing but peanut butter, I guess some things will always stay fantasies.

Too Much Quality Time with Your Kids

From the moment your baby is born and the nurse wipes away that yucky waxy buildup stuff, you hold them in your arms and wonder how you could ever love anyone more. You revel in their every move and stare at them all day as if they were a roaring fire. But then they get older and throw food in your face, and take a dump on your mother-in-law's new carpet during a potty-training regression, and you start counting the days to kindergarten. Once your kids are in school, you revel again, but this time, you revel in the fact that your house can stay clean for more than two consecutive hours.

Yes, parents love having their kids in school. But now that the holidays are upon us, it's time for school break, and you're one step away from having a break yourself—a break *down* that is. Unlike summer vacation where there's camp to go to and summer school to attend, now they're home for up to three weeks straight! On top of that, you have relatives in town, and these relative brought their own kids who are also on winter break. If there's one thing that drives you crazier than your own kids, it's other people's kids. They don't follow the rules and they forget to pick up after themselves. Actually, in those ways, they're a lot like your own kids, only you can't yell at them no matter how much you really want to.

Sure, come December 25, they'll have lots of new toys to play with to keep them busy, but until that time, what are we going to do with these overactive tots to keep them entertained, and more important, off our backs, until their hyperactivity medication kicks in? Here are some ideas:

Let them make decorations. Christmas is a time for crafts, and with a bag full of cheap knickknacks like felt, glitter, glue, old magazines, and safety scissors, your kids can cut and paste their way to making sparkly snowflakes, festive placemats, or colorful ornaments. Go to activitiesforkids .com for some ideas. Be sure to put newspaper underneath the craft table for easy cleanup.

Have your kids help out in the kitchen making baked goods that will be given out as gifts. This is especially helpful if you're not good in the kitchen. No, not because the little rugrats can give you some pointers, but they'll be the perfect excuse when your gingerbread men look like they've just been released from a POW camp. Anyone that hears that the gift was made by tiny fingers is guaranteed to say "awwww!"

If you live in a big city, log on to gocitykids.com. There you'll find a huge array of kid-friendly things to see and do . . . some of which may even be fun for you!

Before the vacation begins, head over to your local video rental shop and load up on holiday favorites. One of the best traits of youngsters is their ability to watch the same program over and over and over again. And these days, with video stores not penalizing for late returns, you don't have the stress of having to return them in two days or else pay more on late fees than the DVD is worth.

Sure it may be stressful to have a house full of kids during the holidays, but if you have enough items on hand, and enough alcohol in the other hand, it may not be too bad. Besides, other people's kids often mean other parents, and if these parents are trustworthy and responsible, perhaps you can even go take a break and go out for a couple of hours by yourself. If they're not trustworthy, just make it twenty minutes.

Chapter 9

it's beginning to smell a lot like christmas

The holidays are full of moments that awaken our senses.
We hear a bell jingle and we envision Santa Claus riding on
his sleigh. We feel the crunch of snow beneath our feet and
reflect on a white Christmas. We see "sale" signs and imagine our wallets being sucked dry. But the strongest holiday
sensation has got to be the wonderful smells that permeate
from your kitchen this time of year. Whether it be gingerbread cookies, turkey with all the fixings, or fumes from
your fire extinguisher as you put out a small grease fire (hey,
we can't all be five-star chefs), the aromas that come from
your kitchen directly connect you with the holidays.

During Christmas, your oven works harder than Ryan
Seacrest. Between the cookie baking, the party preparations,
and the elaborate holiday feasts, there's a lot of work ahead
of you. You've finally cleaned up after Thanksgiving and
now you have to start all over again! If you like to cook,

being in the kitchen all day may not be such a bother. You have all the pots and pans and kitchen gadgets you'll need, and better yet, know how to use them. Got a Cuisinart? Yup. A Mixmaster? Uh huh. A $2 microplaner that you picked up at the hardware store because you know it zests better than the $20 number from the trendy kitchen supply store? Of course. Wow! You really *do* know your stuff! But, for those less fortunate in the kitchen milieu, who don't give a chiffonade about cooking, and who don't understand that joke because you don't know what chiffonade means, cooking for the holidays is going to be a big chore.

Luckily there's a way to turn lemons into festive holiday lemon squares. There are shortcuts to know and secrets to reveal that'll better enable you to make wonderful party food and create sensational suppers without breaking a nail or a small appliance. Yes, after reading this next chapter, you'll find the strength to venture into your kitchen again and sail through the holidays with one spatula tied behind your back.

What's Cookin'? Not a Damn Thing!

Sure, there are people who spend hours in the kitchen creating homemade treats that rival anything seen at Dean and Deluca. They present platters of delectable morsels and watch their guests salivate and cheer their meals for months to come. But is it fair to neglect those who prefer to buy their food premade and deny them such an experience? Well, yeah, it kinda is. But even though it's fair, doesn't mean it has to be the case. These days anyone can present a beautiful tray of appetizers and a buffet table full of magnificent entrees and pass them off for homemade, and no one will be the wiser.

That's because we live in an age of opulence that overflows onto the shelves of our supermarkets. These days you can buy an entire meal fit for company, including plenty of premade treats. Is it going to cost more? Hell yeah. But is it going to save you time, effort, headaches, and stress? You betcha! And that's worth a lot right there. Besides, with these handy-dandy tricks, no one will be able to tell that you didn't make the food from scratch, and you know your secret's safe with me because, well, I don't know who the hell you are.

So, for the sake of your sanity, here are some ways to make store-bought goodies look like homemade:

Use fresh garnish. Any store-bought entrée will look like you spent hours cooking it if you just BAM! it with a handful of chopped, flat leaf parsley or a complimentary herb.

If you buy an oil-based dip like hummus, bruschetta, tapenade, or eggplant spread, give it a homemade look by drizzling it with extra olive oil and sprinkling it with a touch of paprika, roasted pine nuts, or herbs for an added pizzazz!

Decorate the platter. Put a store-bought entrée on a plain platter and surround it with fresh sage leaves and kumquats or fresh cranberries and mini apples. It's like putting a so-so picture in an extraordinary frame.

Toss some small roasted nuts over anything from canned string beans to bagged lettuce. A few classics are toasted almonds, walnuts, pine nuts, or even sesame seeds.

Not only do a few slices of lemons or limes brighten up any platter and make store-bought fish look like you cooked it yourself, but you can also use citrus in drinks. Add a few slices to a pitcher of premade cosmos or iced tea. Toss in a sprig of mint and it's a double whammy!

If you have a very special occasion, you can order specialty items from a catalog. You can get anything from Maryland crab cakes to prepared Cornish game hens. Better yet, get some Southern biscuits still in dough form and bake them off yourself! Your house will smell great, and I defy anyone to tell the difference. These gourmet food items are the cubic zirconia of the culinary world.

Buy plain sugar cookies and those colored tubes of royal icing that you can find where the canned frosting is sold. It works much better than the icing you make yourself because it doesn't squirt out of your plastic baggie and all over the cookie.

Any pie or cake will look homemade if you top it with fresh whipped cream. For an even nicer one though, sprinkle it with cookie crumbs or fresh berries!

Even though your meal may be store-bought, make your house smell great with a pot of mulled cider. Just pour a few gallons of cider into a pot, add cloves and cinnamon sticks, and start simmering it about a half hour before your guests arrive. If you don't like cider, grill up a pan of chopped garlic and onions. If it's a dessert party, bake off a sheet of store-bought cookie dough. If you want your guests to think you cooked, you have to make the house smell good.

An Ounce of Prevention Is Worth a Pound of Cured Meat

Why is it that things always go wrong just when you need them the most? The cable goes out just as Tom Bergeron reveals the Dancing with the Stars winner. Or your groom's "equipment" fails after he had too much to drink at his own wedding. But the biggest frustration of all, next to the honeymoon thing—or the Dancing with the Stars thing if you've been married for a while—is when a kitchen appliance breaks down right when you're in the middle of making a big holiday meal.

When this happens, your first instinct is to bury your head in your hands and cry, "Why me?" But it's really no coincidence that an appliance goes kerpow during December. After all, it's been used more than one of *The Girls Next Door*. With so much food to make, you've overloaded your garbage disposal, washed a week's worth of dishes in one day, and kept your oven on so long you could cure a cow's worth of beef jerky. Wow, you're really going all out for your guests.

Not only can't you use your kitchen, but if anything breaks during the mad holiday rush, it's nearly impossible to get a repair guy to come over and fix it. Even if you can, it'll cost you a fortune, since holiday time means overtime! So, in hopes of avoiding a kitchen disaster that can spoil the fun, and possibly the food, here are some basics tips to keeping your appliances in tip-top shape:

Garbage disposal tips: Know the no-nos of what you can and can't put in there. The major no-nos are bones, grease, potato skins, hamburger, egg shells, anything fibrous like asparagus, lettuce, artichokes, celery, onions, and corn cobs, and any nonfood items like cigarette butts, plastic, and metal. You should also avoid putting a lot of starchy things in there like pasta, rice, and large amounts of potato. After using the garbage disposal, run the water for thirty seconds to make sure that everything has been washed away. To clean the blades, run the disposal and throw in some ice cubes to scrape away any built up gunk. If your garbage disposal does stop, press the red reset button on the bottom, cross your fingers, and say a little prayer to the "fix-it" gods!

Dishwasher tips: Check out the holes in the spray arms. Over time they can get clogged with food debris and bits of plastic. If they are, clean them with the pointy part of a paper clip. Also, be sure that the soap dispenser closes. If it doesn't because there is build up around the edges of the dispenser, be sure to clean it or the soap won't be able to get out to clean the dishes. And finally, if you going to go for an extended period of time without using your dishwasher, pour about an ounce of cooking oil in the puddle of the standing water at the bottom of the machine. This will prevent the water from evaporating and drying out the rubber parts.

Oven tips: My best oven tip is to place a thermometer that can go up to at least 350 degrees on the rack in your oven. Then turn on your oven to 350 and let it preheat for a good ten minutes. Remove the thermometer, and read the temperature. If your oven is off by more than a few degrees, your oven thermostat will need to be fixed or replaced. It's best to try this tip several weeks before the holidays so there'll be ample time to make repairs. If you can't get it fixed beforehand, or the price to fix it is too high, adjust your oven setting to compensate (for instance, if your thermometer only read 300 instead of 350, set your oven 50 degrees hotter).

Refrigerator tip: Every few months, unplug your fridge, pull it away from the wall, and vacuum the coils. Then, pull out the drip pan that's located underneath and clean that as well. A clean fridge takes less effort to run so not only will it work better, but it will also work longer.

Clogged sink tip: Get out your handy-dandy plunger. If you have a double-sided sink, block off the nonclogged side with the sink stopper. Hold down the stopper while you plunge the clogged side until it's cleared. Put the plunger away and sterilize your sink and your hands within an inch of your life. You don't know where that plunger's been—actually you do, which is why you need to sterilize everything!

Bacteria tip: I know bacteria isn't an appliance, but it's a worthy tip nonetheless. Nothing will make your party as memorable as giving your guests a batch of e-coli poisoning as a lovely parting gift. To avoid this kitchen disaster, use separate cutting boards for meats and veggies. Wash your hands and counters thoroughly after touching raw meat, as well as anything you may have touched with your yucky hands before you washed them. And just so you know, your sink has more bacteria than your toilet bowl, so if anything falls in there, don't just fish it out and stick it on a platter! Sanitize your sink often to keep bacteria under control.

Overall tip: Get a good home fix-it book so that you're not helpless when things go wrong. Sure, you'll feel empowered being able to fix all the crap in your home. But the real benefit is not having to rely on repair men which, during the holidays, are as hard to find as someone who would let Michael Vick dog-sit when they're away.

It's My Party and I'll Die If I Want To

Did you ever wonder why it's customary to bring the hostess a nice gift when you arrive at the party? It's because you know that for days the poor thing has been running herself ragged doing all the shopping, cooking, and cleaning, only to spend the majority of the party stressing and sweating and slaving over hot appetizers and cold buffets while her guests have a grand old time. Then, after the guests have driven home and tucked themselves into bed, she'll be up washing the dishes and pretreating red wine stains on her new sisal rug. She deserves a damn vanilla candle for all her trouble.

If you're hesitant about throwing a party because you know how much work it takes, think again. It's actually possible to have a great party, and enjoy it at the same time! You just need to plan ahead and pick a menu that can be prepared in advance. Make a schedule and do as many things as you can ahead of time, and as many days ahead as you can do them. Some early tasks include cleaning the house, setting the table, and washing the napkins and tablecloth if it's a fancy shindig. Make an organized shopping list by grouping together items that are located together at the market (dairy, meat, dry goods, produce). This may seem a bit anal, but it'll help you get everything on your list. The only thing worse than going to the market is having to go back because you forgot something. You can even prep the food early. Chop the veggies ahead of time and store them in Ziplock containers. Also, be sure to pick your outfit a few days in advance as well so you won't have to go through your entire closet an hour before the party only to find you have nothing to wear. Try on your outfit to make sure it fits and that it's not stained with pudding (if you have kids, you'll know exactly what I mean).

Most importantly, pick a menu that's low maintenance. Stick with items that can be made in advance or served at room temperature like quiche or salad (see the resource section for menu ideas). Other easy items are ones that can be prepped in the morning and cooked slowly all day. When it comes to food, take shortcuts like buying a jar of preminced garlic or bottled sauces. Get a few store-bought appetizers and sides to mix in with the homemade dishes. I guarantee your guests won't have a better time if you're stuck in the kitchen making everything from scratch during the party.

On the day of the event, do what needs to be done in the order in which it needs to be done. Start on your appetizers so if, heaven forbid, your guests arrive early, you'll have something to feed them. Ask a close friend to come early in order to have an extra set of hands around because you're husband is still busy sitting on his ass. And don't get dressed too soon or too late. Too soon, and you have to worry about the pudding thing. Too late and you run the risk of being caught in your bathrobe when the doorbell rings.

It's also a fun idea to have your guests help. When they arrive, give each one a cute little note with their assignment for the night. Have someone be in charge of music so there's always something good playing. Another guest can be sure to keep the ice bucket full. You can even assign someone the task of flipping on the coffee pot before sitting down to dinner so the coffee's ready for dessert. The less things for you to do and remember, the less crazed you'll be, and the more time you'll have to enjoy the party.

If you're organized, pick the right menu, and have some help, you can actually enjoy yourself. And if your guests give you a scented candle, stash it on your "hostess gift shelf" and give it to the hostess of the next party you're invited to. Chances are she won't be as prepared as you and will be far more deserving. Plus, it'll be one less errand to do in the future, and that's even more reason to celebrate!

Damn That Martha for Making It Look So Easy!

Around the holidays, it's hard not to feel pressure to serve picturesque meals and host seamless parties. No longer are people impressed by a simple roasted turkey. Now it takes one that's brined in maple syrup and served up on a vintage platter surrounded by baby persimmons picked from your own orchard. No longer can dessert just be a store-bought pumpkin pie. Now, if the dessert isn't a homemade pumpkin mousse with fresh brandy cream swirls, then you may as well serve nothing at all.

> "I don't know why people throw parties.
> The last one I had I spent so much time and money,
> I could have spent a weekend in Santa Barbara. Now I just treat
> myself to a weekend in Santa Barbara and call it a day."
>
> —Leslie

Yes, because of professionals like Martha Stewart, the bar has been lifted when it comes to entertaining. And it's been lifted so high that it's out of reach for many women, especially shorter ones like myself whose feet barely touch the floor when we sit on the toilet. In fact, many people choose not to entertain at all because they feel their party-giving skills won't be enough. They don't feel confident enough to pull off meals with complicated sauces and unpronounceable ingredients or table settings where the napkins must be folded into intricate origami swans and plates must be enhanced with complimentary colored chargers. These women can't create calligraphy place cards or arrange centerpieces with a combination of fresh flowers, fruit, and handmade marzipan sculptures, so they choose to do nothing at all.

So what's a pressure filled hostess to do? First of all, relax. So what if Martha can pull together a Christmas fête worthy of a photo shoot? You know she has an entire staff folding those napkins and arranging those flowers. The only "staff" you have is your husband (yeah, right!) and your kids (double yeah, right!). And even though you feel the pressure to pull off the party of the year, none of your guests really cares. When was the last time you went to a party and were disappointed because the cashews weren't mixed with warm rosemary oil? Puh-leeze! Your guests are just happy to see you, and even more thrilled that they don't have to cook that night.

That being said, there are some easy tips to kick your party up a notch with very little effort on your part, or on the part of husband and kids (I still get a giggle out of that one!):

- Make sure there's festive music playing when your guests arrive. That'll provide an instant mood lift to everyone who walks through your door.
- Have the house smell nice. Usually this comes from what you're cooking, but if you're serving cold or store-bought food, use plug-in scents or candles.
- Have a fire burning. Nothing sets an atmosphere better than a roaring fire. Your guests can smell it burning even before they step in your house. If you don't have a fireplace, light a bevy of candles.
- When it comes to alcohol, make things simple. Beer, wine, and one specialty drink will be perfect. If you want it holiday themed, hang a small candy cane on the edge of the glass.
- Dim the lights. If you don't have a dimmer, install one. If that's too above your comfort level, replace high-watt bulbs with low-watt ones, use strings of tree lights, or burn a lot of candles.
- Don't kill yourself making a lot of difficult hors d'oeuvre. Just make a lot of two or three that are easy to prepare, or get ones that are store bought.
- Forget the complicated pumpkin mousse. Whenever you can't do something fancy, think simple. What about a silver tray stacked high with candy bars?
- If your pets are loud or high maintence, put them in a closed-off room. Same holds true for your kids.

The Most Fearsome of Feasts

You've baked the treats for your kid's school party. You've entertained guests at your open house. And you've made enough cookies to give those Keebler elves a run for their money. So now can you finally throw in the tea towel and call it a day? Absolutely no-can-do. Pace yourself and work through the pain because you still have the Superbowl of suppers to prepare. The homerun of holiday meals! It's Christmas Eve dinner, people! It's more than just a meal. It's an event. A pressure filled event that rings in the beginning of Christmas like nothing else before it. Tradition must be followed to the letter and the food must be cooked with perfection. If one string bean is out of place, one lump in the mashed potatoes, you'll put a blemish on the holidays that's bigger than the one on Nanny McPhee's chin.

If you have company coming, it adds a whole new dimension to the stress level. Not only will you ruin your own family's meal, but others' as well! Sure, they'll pretend the meat isn't dry or that the new flavor in the stuffing is out of this world, but down deep they'll be disappointed because the continuity of the holidays has been broken.

That's why, when it comes to important meals like Christmas Eve dinner, it's best to stick with tradition. It's not the time to swap out your great grandma's ham glaze for a new recipe from Bobby Flay, no matter how much you love poblano chilis. You also shouldn't replace Aunt Gertie's china serving dishes for those trendy Moroccan ones you picked up at Pier One. Everything on the dinner table should be just like as it was the year before, and the year before that. When it comes to things like memorable family meals and sexual positions after a few years of marriage, people stick with what they know.

After your big meal is finished and the dishes are washed and put away, there's still no rest for the weary. You have to help your kids put out cookies and grass clippings for Santa and his reindeer. You have to read them "'Twas the Night Before Christmas." And you have to wrap up the last of Santa's gifts so it looks like he projectile vomited toys underneath the tree come Christmas morning. For heaven's sake, this is Christmas Eve—the final stomping ground before the big day arrives.

the big day!

Congratulations: It's Christmas morning! You've made it across the finish line of what can only be called the holiday Iron Man marathon. You've put up the decorations, fought the traffic, waited in the lines, bought the gifts, wrapped the gifts, mailed the gifts, argued with the spouse, contemplated divorce, bought more gifts for people who got you something that you had nothing for, wrapped more presents, got kissed by a coworker at the office party, met with legal regarding said kiss, and cooked more meals than Wolfgang Puck at the post-Oscars party! You're exhausted and sore and totally spent—and you haven't even gotten out of bed yet. So rise and shine because there are still plenty of holiday hiccups to deal with. If your day is anything like mine, here are a few more circles you have to jump through as your day unfolds:

5:57 A.M.: Your little kids race into your bedroom, jump on your chest, and yell, "Santa came! Santa came!" They've seen the presents underneath the tree, and there ain't no way they're going to wait for you to have your morning coffee and put on your face.

5:59 A.M.: You stumble out of bed and stub your toe hard on the nightstand because the freakin' sun isn't even up yet.

6:01 A.M.: Holy crap! You forgot to dispose of the cookies and lawn clippings your kids left out for Santa and his reindeer. You wolf down both before your kids see and pray that the brown bits on the grass is dirt, and not specks of the dog's business.

6:06 A.M.: You pose together in front of the tree for your annual family portrait. Once again, only a sliver of your head is in frame since you can't figure out the "delay" feature since, hell, you only use it once a year.

6:08 A.M.: You put on your favorite holiday CD. Silent Night plays. You love that song.

6:11 A.M.: The kids start opening their presents.

6:19 A.M.: All the presents are open.

7:13 A.M.: You finally get that last godforsaken toy out of its box, no easy feat, since each one is held down with plastic ties, woven threads, and strong adhesives that lock them in place like a house bolted onto its foundation.

7:18 A.M.: You realize you don't have enough batteries for all the new toys. With the kids screaming in the background, you race around the house desperately pulling them out of wall clocks and flashlights.

8:16 A.M.: (or about that time since the clocks don't work now that the batteries are removed) The kids are done playing and the first "I'm bored" is heard.

8:30 A.M.: You make a big family breakfast and stuff your face full of pancakes, homemade biscuits, bacon, and eggs.

You want a nap but have a mountain of dirty dishes that's larger than the one in *Close Encounters of the Third Kind*.

10:00 A.M.: A neighbor stops by unexpectedly to bring you a gift. You have nothing for her so you rewrap your new Barefoot Contessa cookbook that your husband finally figured out how much you wanted, and give it to her. Damn!

11:42 A.M.: "Silent Night" is played for the twenty-eighth time. God, you hate that song.

12:30 P.M.: Everyone says they're hungry, so you make lunch. You're still bloated from breakfast, but somehow you manage to eat it.

3:13 P.M.: Sports has been playing for three solid hours now. You wonder if your husband would be equally as understanding if you sat on the effin' sofa all day watching Meg Ryan movies.

3:40 P.M.: You and the kids try to make a gingerbread house but your icing's too thin and the whole thing implodes on itself like demolition day on *Extreme Home Makeover*.

6:32 P.M.: Time for Christmas dinner. Between eating breakfast, lunch, and the gingerbread house (what? You can't let something like that go to waste), your belly's bigger than Santa's. You just have a small plate of stuffing. With gravy. And a slice of pie. Gawd, you're in pain!

8:00 P.M.: . . .

The TV is finally off. The guests have dispersed. The kids are sleepy from the lead they've absorbed from their new toys made in China. You sit back and reflect on the day and remember the happy look on your children's faces as they opened the gifts they desperately wanted, and the surprise hug you got from your mother-in-law because you remembered she didn't like nuts in her brownies. You admire your beautiful macaroni necklace your preschooler made for you, and are excited to look over your new cookbook to check out the Contessa's chicken recipe . . . oh crap . . . guess not.

Sure, tomorrow you'll be out there again, fighting the crowds at the after Christmas sale, and crying when you see how cheap everything you bought has become. But as Vivian Leigh said, "Tomorrow's another day." For now, you think about how, when you add together all the pains of Christmas with the joys and laughter and memories you shared with your friends and family, you actually come out ahead. Way ahead in fact. Yes, despite the extreme hassles you've been through all month long, Christmas actually turned out to be a great day after all. An absolutely wonderfully terrific day!

Perhaps the true magic of Christmas is that, despite all the hardships and frustrations, the fighting and the stress, that being with loved ones, reenacting traditions and creating new ones, actually triumphs over all the bad. And that despite everything, Christmas really is . . . the most wonderful time of the year!

On that note, I'd like to say from the bottom of my heart, and the tips of my overworked typing fingers, a merry Christmas to all, and to all a good night!

Resources

Low-maintenance meals to serve at parties:

- Anything braised that can cook slowly all day
- Anything that can be cooked in a slow cooker
- Soups that can be prepared ahead of time and then simply reheated
- Casseroles that can be assembled early and then cooked before guests arrive
- Salads. Don't toss with dressing until the last minute
- Anything that can be served at room temperature
- Antipasto

Cooking Emergency? Call:

Turkey hotline: 1-800-BUTTERBALL

Jennifer's yummy crab dip:

1. Cook 1 cup of chopped onions, chopped bell peppers, and 1 tablespoon minced garlic in a tablespoon of olive oil for about 3 minutes. Remove from heat.

2. Combine 1 pound of room-temperature cream cheese, 1 cup mayo, 1 tablespoon lemon juice, 1 teaspoon salt, and 1 tablespoon Creole seasoning in food processor and process until smooth.

3. Put the mixture in a casserole dish, mix in veggies, and 1 pound lump crab. Cover with ½ cup breadcrumbs that have been mixed with 2 tablespoons melted butter, and cook in a 350-degree oven for about 30 minutes. (This can be assembled ahead of time and baked off before guests arrive).

Web sites to buy personal gifts:

Stamps.com: turn a photo into a real postage stamp.

Shutterfly.com: great Web site to create photo albums, keepsakes, even a deck of cards made with a personal photo.

Threedesigningwomen.com: great for personal stamps and embossers.

Planetjill.com: great jewelry that includes photos of loved ones (or loved pets).

Sneakers: personalized from Nike.com. You choose colors, design, and even write a message.

Skymall.com: you can get someone a puzzle of their neighborhood in an aerial shot (type in "puzzle" in their search box).

Rules for the Party Game of White Elephant:

1. Every guest at the party must bring a wrapped, loser gift they've been given and put it in a pile.
2. Decide on an order (pick numbers from a hat, go from youngest to oldest, drunkest to most sober, who cares, just pick an order).
3. The first person opens a gift of choice.
4. Then, the next person can either take the gift that's opened, or choose another gift. The third person does the same, and the cycle continues until all gifts are opened.

There are variations so if you want to learn more, search Wikipedia or Google for the rules.

About the Author

In addition to the *Sucks* series, **Joanne Kimes** has written for children's and comedy televison shows and magazine articles. She begrudgingly celebrates Christmas with her husband, Jeff, and their daughter, Emily. They live in Studio City, CA. Visit Joanne at *www.sucksandthecity.com*.